Cooking Light.

PASTA
COOKBOOK

Cooking Light®

PASTA
COOKBOOK

COMPILED AND EDITED BY
SUSAN M. McINTOSH, M.S., R.D.

Oxmoor House®

Library of Congress Control Number: 00-136674
ISBN: 0-8487-2492-5
Printed in the United States of America
Second Printing 2001

Previously published as *Low-Fat Ways to Cook Pasta*
  © 1995 by Oxmoor House, Inc.

Editor-in-Chief: Nancy J. Fitzpatrick
Editorial Director, Special Interest Publications: Ann H. Harvey
Senior Foods Editor: Katherine M. Eakin
Senior Editor, Editorial Services: Olivia Kindig Wells
Art Director: James Boone

COOKING LIGHT® PASTA COOKBOOK

Menu and Recipe Consultant: Susan McEwen McIntosh, M.S., R.D.
Copy Editor: Catherine Hamrick
Editorial Assistants: Kelly Hooper Troiano, Julie A. Cole
Assistant Foods Editor: Kathryn Matuszak, R.D.
Indexer: Mary Ann Laurens
Assistant Art Director: Cynthia R. Cooper
Designers: Carol Damsky, Rita Yerby
Senior Photographer: Jim Bathie
Photographers: Howard L. Puckett, Ralph Anderson
Senior Photo Stylist: Kay E. Clarke
Photo Stylists: Cindy Manning Barr, Virginia R. Cravens
Production and Distribution: Phillip Lee
Production Manager: Gail Morris
Associate Production and Distribution Manager: John Charles Gardner
Associate Production Manager: Theresa L. Beste
Production Assistant: Marianne Jordan

Cover: *Pasta with Roasted Peppers and Basil (Recipe follows on page 92)*
Frontispiece: *Turkey-Noodle Casserole (Recipe follows on page 67)*

We're Here for You!

We at Oxmoor House are dedi-
cated to serving you with reliable
information that expands your
imagination and enriches your life.
We welcome your comments and
suggestions. Please write to us at:

Oxmoor House, Inc.
Editor, *Cooking Light®
Pasta Cookbook*
2100 Lakeshore Drive
Birmingham, AL 35209

For more books to enrich your life, visit
oxmoorhouse.com

CONTENTS

PASTA PRIMER

*P*asta—everyone loves it! It's naturally low in fat and sodium and loaded with complex carbohydrates. Pasta cooks quickly and mixes well with other ingredients. Its various shapes and sizes make meals more enticing. And dry pasta is one of the most versatile and convenient foods in the supermarket because it keeps almost indefinitely when stored in an airtight container in a cool, dry place.

PASTA NUTRITION

Health experts are urging us to eat more complex carbohydrates—a source of high energy, starch, and fiber. Isn't it nice, for a change, to be told to eat more of something, not less?

Complex carbohydrates contain—gram for gram—the same number of calories as protein but only one-half the calories of fat. Complex carbohydrates are the main sources of dietary fiber, an important part of a healthy diet.

Complex carbohydrates are different from simple carbohydrates found in a variety of sugars such as table sugar, corn syrup, and honey. Simple carbohydrates also provide energy, but do not contain the beneficial fiber found in complex carbohydrates. (Fruit, vegetables, whole grains, and milk contain both types of carbohydrates.)

Nutritionists recommend that adults eat six servings of pasta, breads, rice, and cereals and at least five servings of fruits and vegetables daily—all sources of complex carbohydrates.

Pasta, a popular source of complex carbohydrates, satisfies the appetite yet is low in sodium, fat, and calories. One-half cup of plain cooked pasta has only 105 calories.

The wide variety of pasta recipes in this book will make it easy for you to increase your servings of complex carbohydrates.

AT THE SUPERMARKET

Pasta is available in about as many shapes and sizes as there are ways to prepare it. Whether you choose dried, fresh, or frozen pasta, the nutritional value is similar, and all contain little fat.

Dried pastas are favorites because they are inexpensive and have a long shelf life. Fresh pasta is made with eggs and flour and cooks very quickly (in 2 minutes or less). You'll find it in the refrigerated section at the supermarket or in specialty stores. You may even want to try your hand at preparing fresh pasta. (Look for recipes and step-by-step instructions beginning on page 10.)

The most common forms of pasta are spaghetti and macaroni, but even these two types take on different looks. Spaghetti comes in a variety of thicknesses, each with a different name, whereas macaroni may appear short, long, straight, or curved. Then there are sea shells, corkscrews, and bow ties, just to name a few.

Be adventurous, and try some of the more intriguing shapes and flavors. Short pasta shapes, such as ziti, shells, and radiatore, are not only easier to eat than their long-stranded counterparts, but their curves and indentations also capture and hold sauces more easily. These small pastas are interchangeable in recipes, as long as you substitute a similar size and thickness.

PASTA POINTERS

To a cook who is short on time, pasta is a reliable staple. While you wait for the water to boil, start preparing the sauce or topping. As the pasta cooks, finish the other dishes you plan to serve.

Here are a few tips to remember when cooking pasta.

• A bundle of long pasta about the diameter of a quarter weighs 4 ounces.

• Use a large Dutch oven or stockpot so that the pasta can move freely in the boiling water. This allows it to cook more evenly.

• Use 4 to 6 quarts of boiling water to cook 1 pound of pasta.

• It is not necessary to add salt or oil to the water; we omitted both in these recipes to avoid adding sodium and fat. For subtle flavor, add fresh lemon juice to the water.

• Bring the water to a rolling boil, and gradually add the pasta so that the water will continue to boil. Once all the pasta has been added, stir and begin timing. Continue to stir occasionally during cooking.

• Cooking times vary, depending on the shape and thickness of the pasta. Begin checking for doneness after the minimum recommended cooking time. Remove a piece of pasta from the water, and bite into it; perfectly cooked pasta will have a tender but slightly firm consistency. This is called "al dente," the Italian phrase for "to the tooth."

• If you're using pasta in a casserole, undercook it during the boiling stage so it will not overcook when baked.

• While pasta itself is generally low in fat, the popular toppings and sauces of butter, cheese, cream, and oil can turn pasta into a high-fat food. Check the nutrition labels on commercial pasta sauces to determine which are low in fat and sodium. Better yet, make your own. In the following chapters, you'll find several delicious low-fat sauce recipes, including classic Marinara Sauce (page 42) and the traditional Bolognese Sauce (page 39).

• Refrigerate leftover pasta in an airtight container for up to 1 week or freeze it for up to a month. To reheat, run hot water over the pasta or place it in a microwave-safe bowl, cover, and microwave at HIGH for 30 seconds to 1 minute.

• You can give most pasta dishes a whole new look by using a different shape; however, you need to try to substitute a pasta that is similar in size and thickness to the one called for in the recipe. Here are some suggestions for appropriate substitutions.

Spaghetti, Thin Spaghetti, or Linguine
Vermicelli or Thin Spaghetti
Elbow Macaroni or Medium Shells
Radiatore or Elbow Macaroni
Wagon Wheels or Elbow Macaroni
Bow Ties or Rigatoni
Ziti or Bow Ties
Mostaccioli, Penne, or Ziti
Rotini, Twists, or Spirals
Orzo, Alphabets, or Ditalini

The many shapes of pasta are identified on pages 8 and 9 in our Guide to Pasta chart.

Pasta Measures Up

Uncooked pasta of similar sizes and shapes may be interchanged in recipes if it is measured by weight, not volume. Cooked pasta, however, should be substituted cup for cup. In general, allow 1 to 2 ounces of uncooked pasta or ½ to 1 cup cooked pasta per person.

Linguine, Spaghetti, or Vermicelli:
  4 ounces dry = 2 to 3 cups cooked
  8 ounces dry = 4 to 5 cups cooked
  16 ounces dry = 8 to 9 cups cooked

Macaroni, Penne, Rotini, or Shells:
  4 ounces dry = 2½ cups cooked
  8 ounces dry = 4½ cups cooked

Fine or Medium Egg Noodles:
  4 ounces dry = 2 to 3 cups cooked
  8 ounces dry = 4 to 5 cups cooked

GUIDE TO PASTA...

ravioli

spaghetti

linguine

tortellini

capellini

fettuccine

bow ties

manicotti

shells

egg noodles

lasagna

spaghettini

vermicelli

From A to Z

FRESH PASTA MADE EASY

*M*aking fresh pasta is not as difficult or time-consuming as you might think. Only 4 ingredients are needed: flour, eggs, salt, and a touch of oil. Prepare the dough by hand or in a food processor. Then roll the dough in a pasta rolling machine, or roll it out by hand.

Most pasta rolling machines have attachments for quickly cutting strips of rolled dough into different widths. If yours doesn't, use a fluted-edged pastry wheel, a plain-edged roller, a pizza cutter, or a sharp knife with a thin blade.

Allow cut pasta to dry 15 to 30 minutes before cooking. Hang it on wooden drying racks, or spread it out on kitchen towels to dry. Handle with care; freshly made pasta dough is delicate.

BASIC PASTA

2 eggs
1 teaspoon olive oil
½ teaspoon salt
1¼ cups plus 1 tablespoon all-purpose flour, divided

Position mixing blade in food processor bowl; add eggs, oil, and salt. Process 30 seconds or until blended. Add 1¼ cups flour; process 30 seconds to 1 minute or until mixture forms a ball.

Sprinkle remaining 1 tablespoon flour evenly over work surface. Turn dough out onto floured surface. Knead dough until smooth and elastic (10 to 15 minutes). Wrap dough in plastic wrap, and let rest 10 minutes. When rolling dough with a pasta machine, work with only 1 portion of the dough at a time. Start by passing the dough through smooth rollers of the machine on the widest setting.

Continue moving the width gauge through narrower settings; pass the dough through rollers once at each setting. Use Basic Pasta dough to create the variations that follow.

Note: Dough may be mixed by hand. Combine 1¼ cups flour and salt; make a well in center of mixture, and set aside. Combine lightly beaten eggs and oil; add to flour mixture, stirring until mixture forms a ball. Turn dough out onto floured surface, and knead as directed above.

CANNELLONI

Divide Basic Pasta dough into 2 equal portions. Working with 1 portion at a time, roll dough to desired thinness (about ⅛ inch). Cut each dough sheet into 7 (5¾- x 5-inch) rectangles. Hang pasta on a wooden drying rack (dry no longer than 30 minutes). Cook pasta in 3 quarts boiling water 2 minutes. Drain. Yield: 14 shells.

PER SHELL: 57 CALORIES (19% FROM FAT)
FAT 1.2G (SATURATED FAT 0.3G)
PROTEIN 2.1G   CARBOHYDRATE 9.0G
CHOLESTEROL 32MG   SODIUM 93MG

FETTUCCINE

Divide Basic Pasta dough into 4 equal portions. Working with 1 portion at a time, roll dough to desired thinness (about 1/16 inch). Pass each dough sheet through fettuccine cutting rollers of machine. Hang pasta on a wooden drying rack (dry no longer than 30 minutes). Cook pasta in 3 quarts boiling water 2 minutes. Drain; serve immediately. Yield: 6 (½-cup) servings.

PER SERVING: 132 CALORIES (19% FROM FAT)
FAT 2.8G (SATURATED FAT 0.7G)
PROTEIN 5.0G   CARBOHYDRATE 21.1G
CHOLESTEROL 74MG   SODIUM 218MG

LASAGNA

Divide Basic Pasta dough into 4 equal portions. Working with 1 portion at a time, roll dough to desired thinness (about 1/16 inch). Cut each dough sheet into 4 (11- x 2-inch) strips. Hang pasta on a wooden drying rack (dry no longer than 30 minutes). Cook pasta in 3 quarts boiling water 2 minutes. Drain. Yield: 16 noodles.

PER NOODLE: 49 CALORIES (18% FROM FAT)
FAT 1.0G (SATURATED FAT 0.3G)
PROTEIN 1.9G   CARBOHYDRATE 7.9G
CHOLESTEROL 28MG   SODIUM 82MG

HOMEMADE PASTA — SOME SAY IT'S BEST

If mixing dough by hand, make a well in the center of dry ingredients; add eggs and oil. Stir until all flour is incorporated. Add seasonings, such as roasted sweet red pepper, curry powder, black pepper, or fresh herbs.

To roll dough by hand, flatten dough with palm of hand. With the rolling pin in center of dough, roll dough away from you, and then rotate dough a quarter-turn. Repeat process until dough is as thin as possible.

Allow dough to dry slightly. Fold dough in thirds lengthwise. If dough sticks when folded over, it has not dried sufficiently. Cut dough into 1/4- to 1/2-inch slices according to desired width, using a sharp knife.

To roll dough using a pasta maker, divide dough into small portions, and flatten each portion into a disc shape. Pass each portion of dough through the smooth rollers of the pasta machine until it becomes a wide, thin sheet.

Adjust the control to the next narrower setting, and feed the entire sheet of dough through the machine, guiding it gently with your hands. Continue narrowing the setting until desired thinness of pasta is achieved.

Select the cutting attachment for desired width of pasta (for spaghetti, linguine, or fettuccine). Pass each sheet of dough through the machine's cutting rollers, gently guiding cut pasta out of cutting rollers.

SWEET PEPPER PASTA

1 large sweet red pepper (½ pound), seeded
    and cut into 1-inch pieces
Olive oil-flavored vegetable cooking spray
1 egg
1 teaspoon olive oil
½ teaspoon salt
1¾ cups unbleached flour

Place pepper pieces in an 11- x 7- x 2-inch baking dish coated with cooking spray. Cover and bake
at 400° for 45 minutes or until peppers are soft, stirring every 15 minutes. Remove from oven; cool.

Position knife blade in food processor bowl; add
pepper pieces. Process until smooth. Add egg, olive
oil, and salt. Process 30 seconds or until mixture is
blended. Add flour, and process 30 seconds to 1
minute or until mixture forms a ball. Process 2 minutes or until smooth and elastic. Wrap in plastic
wrap; let stand 10 minutes. Follow procedure for
Basic Pasta. Yield: 10 (½-cup) servings.

PER SERVING: 87 CALORIES (13% FROM FAT)
FAT 1.3G (SATURATED FAT 0.2G)
PROTEIN 2.9G   CARBOHYDRATE 16.1G
CHOLESTEROL 22MG   SODIUM 125MG

CILANTRO PASTA

1 (4-ounce) can chopped green chiles, drained
2 tablespoons fresh cilantro
1 egg
1 teaspoon olive oil
¼ teaspoon salt
2 cups unbleached flour

Position knife blade in food processor bowl; add
chiles and cilantro. Process until smooth. Add egg,
oil, and salt. Process 30 seconds to 1 minute. Add
flour; process until mixture forms a ball. Process 2
minutes or until smooth and elastic. Cover; let
stand 10 minutes. Follow procedure for Basic Pasta.
Yield: 9 (½-cup) servings.

PER SERVING: 105 CALORIES (11% FROM FAT)
FAT 1.3G (SATURATED FAT 0.3G)
PROTEIN 3.4G   CARBOHYDRATE 19.7G
CHOLESTEROL 25MG   SODIUM 86MG

CURRIED PASTA

2 eggs
1 tablespoon curry powder
1 teaspoon olive oil
½ teaspoon salt
½ teaspoon turmeric
⅛ teaspoon ground red pepper
1½ cups unbleached flour
2 tablespoons water

Position knife blade in food processor bowl; add
first 6 ingredients. Process 30 seconds. Add flour;
process 30 seconds or until mixture forms pea-size
balls. Slowly add water through food chute with
processor running; blend until mixture forms a ball.
Process 2 minutes or until smooth and elastic. Wrap
in plastic wrap; let stand 10 minutes. Follow procedure for Basic Pasta. Yield: 9 (½-cup) servings.

PER SERVING: 91 CALORIES (19% FROM FAT)
FAT 1.9G (SATURATED FAT 0.4G)
PROTEIN 3.6G   CARBOHYDRATE 15.0G
CHOLESTEROL 49MG   SODIUM 146MG

BLACK PEPPER PASTA

2 eggs
1½ to 2 tablespoons coarsely ground pepper
1 teaspoon olive oil
½ teaspoon salt
1½ cups unbleached flour
2 tablespoons plus 2 teaspoons water

Position knife blade in food processor bowl; add
first 4 ingredients. Process 30 seconds or until
blended. Add flour, and process 30 seconds to 1
minute or until mixture forms pea-size balls. Slowly
add water through food chute with processor running, blending until mixture forms a ball. Process 2
minutes or until smooth and elastic. Wrap in plastic
wrap; let stand 10 minutes. Follow procedure for
Basic Pasta. Yield: 9 (½-cup) servings.

PER SERVING: 91 CALORIES (19% FROM FAT)
FAT 1.9G (SATURATED FAT 0.4G)
PROTEIN 3.6G   CARBOHYDRATE 15.2G
CHOLESTEROL 49MG   SODIUM 146MG

LOW-FAT BASICS

*W*hether you are trying to lose or maintain weight, low-fat eating makes good sense. Research studies show that decreasing your fat intake reduces risks of heart disease, diabetes, and some types of cancer. The goal recommended by major health groups is an intake of 30 percent or less of total daily calories.

Cooking Light Pasta Cookbook gives you practical, delicious recipes with realistic advice about low-fat cooking and eating. The recipes are lower in total fat than traditional recipes, and most provide less than 30 percent of calories from fat and less than 10 percent of calories from saturated fat.

If you have one high-fat item during a meal, you can balance it with low-fat choices for the rest of the day and still remain within the recommended percentage. For example, fat contributes 56 percent of the calories in Garden Green Salad for the Saturday Night Spaghetti menu on page 16. However, because the salad is combined with other low-fat foods, the total menu provides only 22 percent of calories as fat.

The goal of fat reduction need not be to eliminate all fat from your diet. In fact, a small amount of fat is needed to transport fat-soluble vitamins and maintain other normal body functions.

FIGURING THE FAT

The easiest way to achieve a diet with 30 percent or fewer of total calories from fat is to establish a daily "fat budget" based on the total number of calories you need each day. To estimate your daily calorie requirements, multiply your current weight by 15. Remember that this is only a rough guide because calorie requirements vary according to age, body size, and level of activity. To gain or lose 1 pound a week, add or subtract 500 calories a day. (A diet of fewer than 1,200 calories a day is not recommended unless medically supervised.)

Once you determine your personal daily caloric requirement, it's easy to figure the number of fat grams you should consume each day. These should equal or be lower than the number of fat grams indicated on the Daily Fat Limits chart.

DAILY FAT LIMITS		
Calories Per Day	30 Percent of Calories	Grams of Fat
1,200	360	40
1,500	450	50
1,800	540	60
2,000	600	67
2,200	660	73
2,500	750	83
2,800	840	93

NUTRITIONAL ANALYSIS

Each recipe in *Cooking Light Pasta Cookbook* has been kitchen-tested by a staff of qualified home economists. Registered dietitians have determined the nutrient information, using a computer system that analyzes every ingredient in any recipe. These efforts ensure the success of each recipe and will help you fit these recipes into your own meal planning.

The nutrient grid that follows each recipe provides calories per serving and the percentage of calories from fat. In addition, the grid lists the grams of total fat, saturated fat, protein, and carbohydrate, and the milligrams of cholesterol and sodium per serving. The nutrient values are as accurate as possible and are based on these assumptions.

• When the recipe calls for cooked pasta, we base the analysis on pasta that has been cooked without additional salt or fat.

• The calculations indicate that meat and poultry are trimmed of fat and skin before cooking.

• Only the amount of marinade absorbed by the food is calculated.

• Garnishes and other optional ingredients are not calculated.

• Some of the alcohol calories evaporate during heating, and only those remaining are counted.

• When a range is given for an ingredient (3 to 3½ cups, for instance), we calculate the lesser amount.

• Fruits and vegetables listed in the ingredients are not peeled unless specified.

SENSIBLE DINNERS

*M*eal planning stymies few cooks once they think of pasta, a good beginning to dinner that only gets better when paired with a green salad or fresh fruit. Add bread—homemade or commercial, depending on time—and, voilà, dinner is served.

Discover plenty of pasta possibilities with these recipes and menu suggestions. Try an easy pasta salad for a mid-week supper or the elegant Burgundy Beef with Parslied Fettuccine (page 26) for a fancy dinner. These and other menu ideas will inspire you to dream up your own variations. With pasta, starting dinner is never a chore, and for your family, the results are pure pleasure.

Spaghetti with Savory Sauce (Menu follows on page 16)

SATURDAY NIGHT SPAGHETTI
(pictured on page 14)

For a hassle-free weekend supper try the following timetable:

Wash the salad greens, and place in a plastic bag or covered container to keep them crisp. Prepare the salad dressing, chill, and add to greens and other vegetables just before the meal. While the spaghetti sauce is simmering, cook the pasta, heat the bread, and make the chocolate sauce. Layer the parfaits just before serving.

Garden Green Salad

Two-Alarm Pepper Bread

Spaghetti with Savory Sauce

Chocolate-Mint Parfaits

Iced Tea

Serves 4
TOTAL CALORIES PER SERVING: 651
(CALORIES FROM FAT: 22%)

GARDEN GREEN SALAD

2 cups torn romaine lettuce
2 cups torn fresh spinach
½ cup sliced green onions
1¾ cups thinly sliced cucumber (about 1 medium)
½ cup thinly sliced celery
8 cherry tomatoes, halved
3 tablespoons white wine vinegar
1 tablespoon vegetable oil
1 teaspoon dried parsley flakes
½ teaspoon sugar
¼ teaspoon dried whole oregano
⅛ teaspoon garlic powder
⅛ teaspoon pepper

Combine first 6 ingredients in a large bowl; toss well. Combine vinegar and remaining ingredients in a jar. Cover tightly, and shake vigorously. Pour dressing over lettuce mixture, and toss gently. Yield: 4 (1½-cup) servings.

PER SERVING: 59 CALORIES (56% FROM FAT)
FAT 3.7G (SATURATED FAT 0.7G)
PROTEIN 1.7G   CARBOHYDRATE 5.8G
CHOLESTEROL 0MG   SODIUM 34MG

TWO-ALARM PEPPER BREAD

4 (1-inch) slices French bread
1 tablespoon reduced-calorie margarine, melted
1 teaspoon dried parsley flakes
⅛ teaspoon crushed red pepper
Dash of coarsely ground pepper

Place bread slices on an ungreased baking sheet. Combine margarine and remaining ingredients in a small bowl; brush top side of each bread slice with margarine mixture. Bake at 350° for 10 minutes or until thoroughly heated. Serve bread warm. Yield: 4 servings.

PER SERVING: 139 CALORIES (17% FROM FAT)
FAT 2.7G (SATURATED FAT 0.5G)
PROTEIN 3.9G   CARBOHYDRATE 23.7G
CHOLESTEROL 1MG   SODIUM 275MG

SPAGHETTI WITH SAVORY SAUCE

Vegetable cooking spray
1 pound freshly ground raw turkey
3 tablespoons minced onion
2 cups water
1½ teaspoons dried Italian seasoning
¼ teaspoon garlic powder
⅛ teaspoon salt
1 (6-ounce) can no-salt-added tomato paste
4 ounces spaghetti, uncooked
1 tablespoon grated Parmesan cheese

Coat a large nonstick skillet with cooking spray; place over medium-high heat until hot. Add turkey and onion; cook over medium heat until turkey is lightly browned, stirring to crumble. Drain and pat dry with paper towels. Wipe drippings from skillet with a paper towel. Add turkey mixture, water, and next 4 ingredients to skillet. Bring to a boil. Reduce heat, and simmer 10 minutes or until thickened, stirring occasionally.

Cook spaghetti according to package directions, omitting salt and fat; drain. Place on a serving platter; top with sauce. Sprinkle with cheese. Yield: 4 (1¼-cup) servings.

PER SERVING: 296 CALORIES (16% FROM FAT)
FAT 5.3G (SATURATED FAT 1.7G)
PROTEIN 30.8G   CARBOHYDRATE 30.3G
CHOLESTEROL 66MG   SODIUM 175MG

CHOCOLATE-MINT PARFAITS

¼ cup plus 2 tablespoons water
3 tablespoons sugar
2 tablespoons unsweetened cocoa
1½ teaspoons cornstarch
¼ teaspoon mint flavoring
2 cups vanilla ice milk
1 tablespoon plus 1 teaspoon finely chopped pecans, toasted
Fresh mint sprigs (optional)

Combine first 4 ingredients in a medium saucepan; stir well. Cook over medium heat, stirring constantly, 8 to 10 minutes or until smooth and thickened. Remove sauce from heat, and stir in mint flavoring.

Spoon ¼ cup ice milk into each of 4 parfait glasses; top each with 1 tablespoon chocolate sauce. Repeat procedure with remaining ice milk and chocolate sauce. Sprinkle 1 teaspoon chopped pecans over each serving. Garnish parfaits with fresh mint sprigs, if desired. Serve immediately. Yield: 4 servings.

PER SERVING: 157 CALORIES (25% FROM FAT)
FAT 4.4G (SATURATED FAT 2.1G)
PROTEIN 3.4G   CARBOHYDRATE 26.9G
CHOLESTEROL 9MG   SODIUM 57MG

Use 4 quarts of water to cook each pound of pasta—the goal is to allow plenty of room for the pasta to move around. Gently push long pasta such as spaghetti into boiling water as the pasta softens. That way, you don't have to break the pasta to fit the pan. Start timing when the water returns to a full boil, and cook the pasta uncovered, stirring occasionally to separate.

Lemon-Chicken Pasta

PASTA FOR TWO

In this quick menu for two, we suggest using bow tie pasta in Lemon-Chicken Pasta, but rotelle or fusilli substitutes nicely.

Lemon-Chicken Pasta
Onion-Spinach Salad
Jumbo Pumpkin Cookies

Serves 2
TOTAL CALORIES PER SERVING: 737
(CALORIES FROM FAT: 22%)

LEMON-CHICKEN PASTA

Vegetable cooking spray
1 teaspoon olive oil
2 cloves garlic, minced
6 ounces skinned, boned chicken breast, cut into ¼-inch-wide strips
½ cup frozen English peas, thawed
⅓ cup coarsely shredded carrot
½ cup low-sodium chicken broth, undiluted
2 tablespoons light process cream cheese
2 cups cooked farfalle (bow tie pasta)
3 tablespoons grated Parmesan cheese
½ teaspoon grated lemon rind
⅛ teaspoon salt
⅛ teaspoon pepper

Coat a large nonstick skillet with cooking spray; add oil. Place over medium-high heat until hot. Add garlic; sauté 15 seconds. Add chicken; sauté 1 minute. Add peas and carrot; sauté 1 minute. Remove from skillet; set aside.

Add broth and cream cheese to skillet; cook over medium-high heat 3 minutes or until cheese melts, stirring constantly with a wire whisk. Stir in chicken mixture, farfalle, and next 4 ingredients; cook 1 minute. Yield: 2 (1½-cup) servings.

PER SERVING: 422 CALORIES (21% FROM FAT)
FAT 9.7G (SATURATED FAT 3.6G)
PROTEIN 33.6G CARBOHYDRATE 48.4G
CHOLESTEROL 63MG SODIUM 478MG

ONION-SPINACH SALAD

½ cup slivered purple onion
3 tablespoons water
3 tablespoons red wine vinegar
1 teaspoon honey
1 teaspoon olive oil
⅛ teaspoon salt
¼ teaspoon pepper
5 cups loosely packed torn fresh spinach

Combine onion and next 6 ingredients in a small skillet; cook over medium-low heat 7 minutes or until onion is crisp-tender. Immediately pour over spinach, tossing gently. Yield: 2 (2-cup) servings.

PER SERVING: 76 CALORIES (33% FROM FAT)
FAT 2.8G (SATURATED FAT 0.4G)
PROTEIN 4.4G CARBOHYDRATE 48.4G
CHOLESTEROL 0MG SODIUM 258MG

JUMBO PUMPKIN COOKIES

⅓ cup all-purpose flour
3 tablespoons sugar
½ teaspoon ground cinnamon
¼ teaspoon baking powder
⅛ teaspoon baking soda
⅛ teaspoon salt
¼ cup mashed cooked pumpkin
2 tablespoons golden raisins
1 tablespoon frozen egg substitute, thawed
1 teaspoon vegetable oil
Vegetable cooking spray
1 tablespoon chopped pecans

Combine first 6 ingredients in a bowl; set aside. Combine pumpkin and next 3 ingredients; add to dry ingredients, stirring just until moistened.

Spoon batter into 2 (3-inch) circles on a baking sheet coated with cooking spray; sprinkle with pecans. Bake at 375° for 17 minutes or until cookies spring back when touched lightly in the center. Yield: 2 cookies.

PER COOKIE: 239 CALORIES (20% FROM FAT)
FAT 5.4G (SATURATED FAT 0.7G)
PROTEIN 3.8G CARBOHYDRATE 45.8G
CHOLESTEROL 0MG SODIUM 239MG

QUICK PASTA FOR COMPANY

This pasta and turkey entrée looks impressive, but actually it's a cinch. English peas, sourdough rolls (one per person), and a peach dessert balance the menu.

Ham-Filled Turkey Rolls with Pasta

English peas

Sourdough rolls

Gingered Peach Crisp

Serves 4
TOTAL CALORIES PER SERVING: 702
(CALORIES FROM FAT: 14%)

HAM-FILLED TURKEY ROLLS WITH PASTA

4 (2½-ounce) turkey breast cutlets
4 ounces thinly sliced lower-salt ham
¼ teaspoon rubbed sage
¼ teaspoon pepper
Vegetable cooking spray
½ cup finely chopped shallots
1 cup Chablis or other dry white wine
½ cup water
2 cups hot cooked capellini (angel hair pasta),
    cooked without salt or fat

Place each cutlet between 2 sheets of heavy-duty plastic wrap. Flatten to ⅛-inch thickness, using a meat mallet or rolling pin. Top each cutlet with one-fourth of ham; sprinkle with sage and pepper. Roll up jellyroll fashion, tucking in sides of cutlet; secure with wooden picks.

Coat a small skillet with cooking spray; place over medium heat until hot. Add turkey rolls, and sauté 3 minutes or until lightly browned. Add shallots; cook 1 minute, stirring constantly. Add wine and water; cook an additional 10 minutes or until turkey rolls are done, turning occasionally. Remove rolls from pan, reserving cooking liquid. Discard wooden picks.

Cut each roll crosswise into ¼-inch slices; arrange over pasta. Drizzle with reserved cooking liquid. Yield: 4 servings.

PER SERVING: 235 CALORIES (12% FROM FAT)
FAT 3.1G (SATURATED FAT 1.2G)
PROTEIN 25.8G   CARBOHYDRATE 24.7G
CHOLESTEROL 56MG   SODIUM 272MG

GINGERED PEACH CRISP

8 gingersnap cookies, crushed
2 tablespoons brown sugar
½ teaspoon ground cinnamon
1 tablespoon margarine
2 (16-ounce) cans peach slices in extra light
    syrup, drained
Vegetable cooking spray
1⅓ cups nonfat vanilla ice cream

Combine crushed gingersnaps, brown sugar, and cinnamon in a bowl; cut in margarine with a pastry blender until mixture resembles coarse meal.

Arrange peaches in an 8-inch square baking dish coated with cooking spray. Sprinkle gingersnap mixture over peaches. Bake at 375° for 20 minutes. For each serving, spoon ¾ cup peach mixture over ⅓ cup ice cream. Yield: 4 servings.

PER SERVING: 303 CALORIES (17% FROM FAT)
FAT 5.7G (SATURATED FAT 1.2G)
PROTEIN 3.4G   CARBOHYDRATE 62.9G
CHOLESTEROL 6MG   SODIUM 97MG

Ham-Filled Turkey Rolls with Pasta

Pasta with Ham and Artichokes

NEIGHBORHOOD SUPPER

Take a break from your fast-paced routines with a friendly get-together. Since the flavor of the cucumber slices and the tea improves with standing, prepare these first. Bake the cake ahead, if desired. Slice pita bread into triangles and toast. Cook the pasta, assemble the entrée, and you're ready. Offer two pita triangles and one piece of cake per serving.

Mississippi River Tea

Pasta with Ham and Artichokes

Cool Cucumber Slices

Toasted Pita Triangles

Strawberry Snack Cake

Serves 4
TOTAL CALORIES PER SERVING: 552
(CALORIES FROM FAT: 15%)

MISSISSIPPI RIVER TEA

2 cups brewed tea
1½ cups unsweetened orange juice
¾ cup unsweetened pineapple juice
5 whole cloves
1 (3-inch) stick cinnamon
¼ teaspoon whole allspice
Orange slices (optional)

Combine first 6 ingredients in a medium saucepan. Bring to a boil. Remove from heat; cover and let stand 20 minutes. Remove and discard spices, using a slotted spoon. Cover and chill. Serve over ice; garnish with orange slices, if desired. Yield: 4 (1-cup) servings.

PER SERVING: 69 CALORIES (1% FROM FAT)
FAT 0.1G (SATURATED FAT 0G)
PROTEIN 0.8G CARBOHYDRATE 16.9G
CHOLESTEROL 0MG SODIUM 5MG

PASTA WITH HAM AND ARTICHOKES

4 ounces tri-color fusilli (corkscrew pasta), uncooked
1 (14-ounce) can artichoke hearts, drained and coarsely chopped
1¼ cups canned garbanzo beans, rinsed and drained
¼ pound lean cooked ham, cut into julienne strips
1 (2-ounce) jar sliced pimiento, undrained
2½ tablespoons Chablis or other dry white wine
2 tablespoons Dijon mustard
1 teaspoon chopped fresh basil
⅛ teaspoon cracked pepper
Fresh basil sprigs (optional)

Cook pasta according to package directions, omitting salt and fat; drain. Rinse with cold water, and drain well. Combine pasta, artichoke hearts, and next 3 ingredients in a bowl; toss gently. Combine wine and next 3 ingredients in a small bowl; stir well. Pour over pasta mixture, and toss gently. Cover and chill. Garnish with basil sprigs, if desired. Yield: 4 (1¼-cup) servings.

PER SERVING: 271 CALORIES (13% FROM FAT)
FAT 3.9G (SATURATED FAT 1.0G)
PROTEIN 15.2G CARBOHYDRATE 42.7G
CHOLESTEROL 13MG SODIUM 670MG

Sodium Alert

The main-dish salad is a little high in sodium due to the ham, canned vegetables, and Dijon mustard. But the other recipes are quite low in sodium so that the menu totals only 885 milligrams. (The American Heart Association recommends adults limit their sodium intake to under 3,000 milligrams a day.)

Cool Cucumber Slices

2 cups thinly sliced cucumber
⅓ cup white wine vinegar
1 tablespoon chopped fresh mint
1 teaspoon sugar
⅛ teaspoon salt
⅛ teaspoon ground white pepper

Place cucumber slices in a medium bowl, and set aside.

Combine vinegar, chopped mint, sugar, salt, and white pepper in a small bowl; stir well.

Pour vinegar mixture over cucumber slices, and toss gently. Cover and chill, stirring occasionally. Serve cucumber slices with a slotted spoon. Yield: 4 (½-cup) servings.

Per Serving: 17 Calories (5% from fat)
Fat 0.1g (Saturated Fat 0g)
Protein 0.5g Carbohydrate 3.4g
Cholesterol 0mg Sodium 79mg

Toasted Pita Triangles

1 (8-inch) pita bread round

Separate pita bread into 2 rounds. Cut each round into 6 pie-shaped pieces; place on an ungreased baking sheet.

Bake pita triangles at 400° for 7 minutes or until lightly browned. Yield: 12 pita triangles.

Per Triangle: 12 Calories (8% from fat)
Fat 0.1g (Saturated Fat 0g)
Protein 0.2g Carbohydrate 2.4g
Cholesterol 0mg Sodium 36mg

Strawberry Snack Cake

1½ cups all-purpose flour
2 teaspoons baking powder
⅛ teaspoon salt
½ cup sugar
½ cup strawberry low-fat yogurt
¼ cup skim milk
3 tablespoons margarine, melted
1 egg, lightly beaten
½ teaspoon vanilla extract
⅔ cup sliced ripe strawberries, slightly mashed
Vegetable cooking spray
1 teaspoon powdered sugar
Strawberry fans (optional)

Combine flour, baking powder, salt, and sugar in a large bowl, stirring well; make a well in center of mixture. Combine yogurt and next 4 ingredients in a bowl; add to dry ingredients. Stir just until dry ingredients are moistened. Gently fold in mashed strawberries.

Spoon batter into an 8-inch square baking pan coated with cooking spray. Bake at 350° for 25 to 30 minutes or until a wooden pick inserted in center comes out clean. Cool in pan 10 minutes on a wire rack. Sprinkle with powdered sugar just before serving, and garnish each square with a strawberry fan, if desired. Yield: 9 servings.

Per Serving: 183 Calories (24% from fat)
Fat 4.8g (Saturated Fat 1.1g)
Protein 3.7g Carbohydrate 31.3g
Cholesterol 25mg Sodium 95mg

ELEGANT PASTA DINNER PARTY

Celebrate the next birthday, graduation, or job promotion with an elegant dinner party for family or friends. For the first course, we suggest a flavorful consommé made with fresh and dried mushrooms. The centerpiece of the dinner is a wonderful stew rich in vegetables, blanketed in a red wine broth and served on a bed of parslied fettuccine. Take a bow for the grand finale, a rich-tasting sorbet, definitely worth the effort.

Wild Mushroom Consommé

Burgundy Beef with Parslied Fettuccine

Plum-Wine Sorbet

Serves 8
TOTAL CALORIES PER SERVING: 608
(CALORIES FROM FAT: 19%)

Burgundy Beef with Parslied Fettuccine

WILD MUSHROOM CONSOMMÉ

12 ounces fresh mushrooms, divided
6 (10½-ounce) cans no-salt-added chicken
    broth, undiluted
2 ounces dried porcini mushrooms
3 tablespoons minced shallots
1 ounce fresh gingerroot, peeled and sliced
¼ teaspoon salt
1 tablespoon dry sherry
1 teaspoon reduced-sodium soy sauce
1¾ ounces fresh enoki mushrooms
1 green onion, thinly sliced

   Slice 4 ounces fresh mushrooms; set aside.
Coarsely chop remaining 8 ounces fresh mushrooms; set aside.
   Place chicken broth in a Dutch oven; bring to a
boil. Add chopped fresh mushrooms, porcini mushrooms, shallots, gingerroot, and salt. Reduce heat,
and simmer, uncovered, 30 minutes, stirring occasionally. Remove from heat. Strain mixture through
a fine sieve; discard mushroom mixture.
   Return strained liquid to Dutch oven. Add sliced
fresh mushrooms, stirring well. Cook over medium
heat 5 minutes. Add sherry and soy sauce; cook 1
minute.
   To serve, ladle soup into individual serving
bowls. Top servings evenly with enoki mushrooms
and green onion slices. Yield: 8 (¾-cup) servings.

PER SERVING: 79 CALORIES (24% FROM FAT)
FAT 2.1G (SATURATED FAT 0.7G)
PROTEIN 3.7G CARBOHYDRATE 9.2G
CHOLESTEROL 0MG SODIUM 223MG

BURGUNDY BEEF WITH PARSLIED FETTUCCINE

2 pounds beef tenderloin
1 cup Burgundy or other dry red wine
2 tablespoons cognac
1 tablespoon black peppercorns
2 bay leaves
1 teaspoon dried whole thyme
1 teaspoon Worcestershire sauce
Vegetable cooking spray
1 tablespoon olive oil
6 ounces pearl onions, peeled
1 cup canned low-sodium beef broth, undiluted
3 medium carrots, scraped and cut diagonally
    into ½-inch pieces
1 (9-ounce) package frozen artichoke hearts
½ pound fresh snow pea pods, trimmed
1 tablespoon cornstarch
1 tablespoon water
¼ teaspoon freshly ground pepper
4 cups hot cooked fettuccine (cooked without
    salt or fat)
1 tablespoon chopped fresh parsley

   Trim fat from beef; cut beef into 1-inch cubes,
and place in a large bowl. Combine wine and next
5 ingredients, stirring well; pour wine mixture over
beef. Cover and marinate in refrigerator 8 hours.
Drain beef, reserving marinade. Set beef aside.
Strain marinade, and set aside.
   Coat a large nonstick skillet with cooking spray;
add olive oil. Place over medium-high heat until
hot. Add half the beef cubes, and cook 5 minutes
or until browned, turning frequently. Remove beef
from skillet, and set aside. Add remaining beef
cubes to skillet, and cook until browned. Remove
beef from skillet, and set aside.
   Add onions to skillet, and sauté 5 minutes or
until tender. Stir in reserved marinade and beef
broth. Bring to a boil; reduce heat, and simmer,
uncovered, 15 minutes. Add carrots, and cook 5
minutes. Add artichoke hearts, and cook 6 minutes.
Add beef cubes, and cook 5 minutes. Add snow
peas, and cook 3 minutes or until crisp-tender.

Combine cornstarch and water, stirring until smooth; stir cornstarch mixture into beef mixture. Add freshly ground pepper, stirring well to combine. Cook until vegetables and meat are tender, and mixture is slightly thickened.

Place fettuccine on a serving platter. Sprinkle parsley over fettuccine, and toss gently to combine. Top with beef mixture. Yield: 8 servings.

PER SERVING: 337 CALORIES (26% FROM FAT)
FAT 9.9G (SATURATED FAT 3.3G)
PROTEIN 28.9G CARBOHYDRATE 29.5G
CHOLESTEROL 70MG SODIUM 94MG

PLUM-WINE SORBET

1 cup sugar
1 cup port wine
1½ pounds plums, pitted and halved
2 tablespoons lemon juice
Fresh mint sprigs (optional)

Combine sugar and wine in a medium saucepan. Bring to a boil; reduce heat, and simmer 5 minutes or until sugar dissolves, stirring occasionally. Remove from heat; let cool.

Position knife blade in food processor bowl; add plums and lemon juice. Process until smooth.

Combine plum mixture and sugar syrup, stirring well. Pour mixture into an 8-inch square pan; freeze until almost firm. Break mixture into large pieces, and place in processor bowl; process until fluffy, but not thawed. Return mixture to pan; freeze until firm.

To serve, scoop sorbet into individual dessert bowls. If desired, garnish each serving with fresh mint sprigs. Yield: 8 (½-cup) servings.

PER SERVING: 192 CALORIES (2% FROM FAT)
FAT 0.5G (SATURATED FAT 0G)
PROTEIN 0.7G CARBOHYDRATE 29.5G
CHOLESTEROL 0MG SODIUM 2MG

Fat Alert

Want to trim the fat from your own pasta recipes? Here are some low-fat substitutes for ingredients frequently added to pasta.

Recipe calls for:	Substitute:
Whole or 2% milk	Skim milk
Whipping cream	Evaporated skimmed milk
Cheddar, American, Swiss, or Monterey Jack cheese	Cheeses with 5 grams of fat or fewer per ounce
Mozzarella cheese	Part-skim mozzarella cheese
Cream cheese	Light cream cheese products; Neufchâtel cheese
Creamed cottage cheese	Nonfat or 1% fat cottage cheese; farmer's cheese
Sour cream	Nonfat or low-fat sour cream; nonfat or low-fat yogurt
Whole egg	2 egg whites or ¼ cup egg substitute
Margarine	Reduce amount, using a margarine made from monounsaturated or polyunsaturated oil; or use reduced-calorie margarine
Vegetable oil	Reduce amount, using a monounsaturated or polyunsaturated oil
Ground beef	Ground turkey or lean ground round
Bacon strips	Turkey bacon or Canadian-style bacon
Poultry	Skinned poultry
Tuna packed in oil	Tuna packed in spring water

PASTA TRADITIONS

*H*ear the word "pasta" and what comes to mind? Spaghetti, lasagna, Fettuccine Alfredo, or everyone's favorite, macaroni and cheese. We've pulled these and many more familiar pasta recipes into one chapter to help you find them easily.

But we have avoided one tradition—the usual load of butter, cream, and cheese—while safeguarding flavor. A creative blend of seasonings and innovative cooking techniques help cut the fat without losing one ounce of tradition.

Pasta Primavera (Recipe follows on page 33)

Fettuccine Alfredo

FETTUCCINE ALFREDO

1 tablespoon margarine
2 small cloves garlic, minced
1 tablespoon all-purpose flour
1⅓ cups skim milk
2 tablespoons light process cream cheese
    product
1¼ cups (2½ ounces) freshly grated Parmesan
    cheese, divided
4 cups hot cooked fettuccine (cooked without
    salt or fat)
2 teaspoons chopped fresh parsley
Freshly ground pepper

Melt margarine in a saucepan over medium heat. Add garlic; sauté 1 minute. Stir in flour. Gradually add milk, stirring with a wire whisk until blended; cook, stirring constantly, 8 minutes or until thickened and bubbly. Stir in cream cheese; cook 2 minutes. Add 1 cup Parmesan cheese, stirring constantly until it melts.

Pour cheese mixture over hot cooked fettuccine; toss well to coat. Top with remaining ¼ cup Parmesan cheese, fresh parsley, and pepper. Yield: 4 (1-cup) servings.

PER SERVING: 345 CALORIES (25% FROM FAT)
FAT 9.7G (SATURATED FAT 4.4G)
PROTEIN 16.8G   CARBOHYDRATE 46.7G
CHOLESTEROL 18MG   SODIUM 401MG

NOODLES ROMANOFF

Vegetable cooking spray
1½ cups sliced fresh mushrooms
2 cloves garlic, minced
2 cups cooked medium egg noodles (cooked
    without salt or fat)
½ cup nonfat sour cream alternative
2 tablespoons chopped green onions
2 tablespoons chopped fresh parsley
¼ teaspoon salt
¼ teaspoon pepper
2 tablespoons grated Parmesan cheese

Coat a large nonstick skillet with cooking spray; place skillet over medium-high heat until hot. Add sliced mushrooms and minced garlic; sauté 3 minutes or until mushrooms are tender. Add noodles and next 5 ingredients to skillet, stirring gently.

Transfer noodle mixture to a 1-quart casserole coated with cooking spray. Top with Parmesan cheese. Bake, covered, at 350° for 20 minutes; uncover and bake an additional 5 minutes or until Parmesan cheese is lightly browned. Yield: 6 (½-cup) servings.

PER SERVING: 101 CALORIES (14% FROM FAT)
FAT 1.6G (SATURATED FAT 0.5G)
PROTEIN 5.1G   CARBOHYDRATE 16.1G
CHOLESTEROL 19MG   SODIUM 148MG

Did You Know?

A fledgling restaurateur is credited with creating Fettuccine Alfredo in 1914 for his pregnant wife, who had little appetite for even his finest dishes. Late one night in his tiny kitchen, Alfredo di Lelio tossed together hot fresh fettuccine with butter and Parmegiano Reggiano cheese, and a pasta classic was born. His wife could not resist the concoction. Soon customers were demanding this recipe sensation, and since that time generations have enjoyed preparing their own Fettuccine Alfredo—only to give it up for low-fat eating. Deprive yourself no more:

• Replace heavy cream with a low-fat white sauce made from skim milk, margarine, and flour.

• Add light cream cheese product to thicken the sauce and to replace the dairy flavor lost when heavy cream is omitted.

• Add minced fresh garlic, a sprinkling of freshly ground pepper, and chopped fresh parsley to enhance the flavor.

• For best results, use fresh Parmesan cheese, and grate just before preparing the dish.

Macaroni and Cheese

MACARONI AND CHEESE

1 (8-ounce) package elbow macaroni,
    uncooked
Vegetable cooking spray
3 tablespoons margarine
¼ cup finely chopped onion
¼ cup all-purpose flour
2 cups evaporated skimmed milk, divided
1½ cups (6 ounces) shredded reduced-fat
    sharp Cheddar cheese
½ teaspoon salt
½ teaspoon dry mustard
¼ teaspoon pepper
¼ cup frozen egg substitute, thawed

Cook macaroni according to package directions, omitting salt and fat; drain well, and set aside.

Coat a medium saucepan with cooking spray; add margarine. Place over medium-high heat until margarine melts. Add onion; sauté until tender. Combine flour and ½ cup milk; stir until smooth. Add flour mixture to onion, stirring well. Add remaining 1½ cups milk to onion mixture. Cook over medium heat, stirring constantly, until mixture is thickened and bubbly. Remove from heat; add cheese and next 3 ingredients, stirring until cheese melts. Gradually stir about one-fourth of hot mixture into egg substitute; add to remaining hot mixture, stirring constantly.

Combine macaroni and cheese sauce; stir well. Pour mixture into a 2-quart casserole coated with cooking spray. Bake at 350° for 30 to 35 minutes or until bubbly. Yield: 10 servings.

PER SERVING: 223 CALORIES (29% FROM FAT)
FAT 7.3G (SATURATED FAT 2.7G)
PROTEIN 12.8G CARBOHYDRATE 26.3G
CHOLESTEROL 13MG SODIUM 350MG

PASTA PRIMAVERA
(pictured on page 28)

8 ounces capellini (angel hair pasta), uncooked
¼ cup reduced-calorie margarine
2 cups sliced broccoli flowerets
1 cup thinly sliced carrot
½ cup sliced green onions
2 cloves garlic, minced
1 tablespoon dried whole basil
2 cups sliced fresh mushrooms
¼ teaspoon salt
¼ teaspoon pepper
½ cup Chablis or other dry white wine
3 tablespoons grated Parmesan cheese

Cook pasta according to package directions, omitting salt and fat. Drain and keep warm.

Place margarine in a large nonstick skillet; place over medium heat until hot. Add broccoli, carrot, onions, garlic, and basil; sauté 5 minutes or until vegetables are crisp-tender, stirring frequently. Add mushrooms, salt, pepper, and wine; cook 2 minutes or until mushrooms are tender. Gently toss pasta with vegetable mixture and Parmesan cheese. Yield: 9 (¾-cup) servings.

PER SERVING: 155 CALORIES (25% FROM FAT)
FAT 4.3G (SATURATED FAT 0.8G)
PROTEIN 5.2G CARBOHYDRATE 22.8G
CHOLESTEROL 1MG SODIUM 159MG

Fat Tip-off

Although the variety of low-fat cheeses is increasing, many weigh in at more than 50 percent fat. Use these tips to decrease the fat in your own recipes:

• Substitute reduced-fat cheeses for higher-fat counterparts.

• Shred or grate cheese to make it go further.

• Decrease the amount of cheese used by one-third to one-half, and substitute a strong-flavored cheese to achieve a full flavor.

LINGUINE WITH CLAM SAUCE

Add a crisp green salad, a favorite vegetable, and crusty Italian bread to this entrée for a simple but tasteful dinner.

6 ounces linguine, uncooked
2 (6½-ounce) cans minced clams
½ pound fresh mushrooms, sliced
2 cloves garlic, minced
1 tablespoon margarine, melted
½ cup chopped fresh parsley
¼ cup Chablis or other dry white wine
¾ teaspoon pepper
⅛ teaspoon salt
¼ cup grated Parmesan cheese

Cook linguine according to package directions, omitting salt and fat; drain. Set aside; keep warm.

Place clams in a colander, and rinse 1 minute; set colander aside to let clams drain.

Sauté mushrooms and garlic in margarine in a large skillet until tender. Stir in clams, parsley, wine, pepper, and salt; simmer, uncovered, until thoroughly heated.

Combine linguine, clam sauce, and Parmesan cheese; toss well. Transfer to a platter and serve. Yield: 4 (1-cup) servings.

PER SERVING: 278 CALORIES (21% FROM FAT)
FAT 6.5G (SATURATED FAT 2.1G)
PROTEIN 17.2G CARBOHYDRATE 37.6G
CHOLESTEROL 25MG SODIUM 278MG

FYI

Most of the alcohol calories in wine evaporate during cooking, leaving only the flavor behind. But you may omit the wine and substitute low-sodium chicken broth or fruit juices such as apple or white grape juice.

LINGUINE WITH RED CLAM SAUCE

This pasta dish is ready in less than 30 minutes. Cook the pasta while the sauce simmers so that both will be done at the same time.

Vegetable cooking spray
¼ cup chopped onion
1 (14½-ounce) can no-salt-added whole tomatoes, undrained and chopped
1 (6-ounce) can no-salt-added tomato paste
¼ cup Chablis or other dry white wine
¼ cup no-salt-added tomato juice
1 teaspoon dried whole basil
½ teaspoon garlic powder
⅛ teaspoon crushed red pepper
1 (10-ounce) can whole baby clams, drained
8 ounces linguine, uncooked
¼ cup grated Parmesan cheese
Fresh basil sprigs (optional)

Coat a large nonstick skillet with cooking spray; place over medium-high heat until hot. Add onion, and sauté until tender. Add chopped tomato and next 6 ingredients; bring to a boil. Reduce heat, and simmer, uncovered, 10 minutes or until sauce is of desired consistency, stirring occasionally. Stir in clams, and cook until thoroughly heated.

Cook linguine according to package directions, omitting salt and fat; drain well. Divide linguine evenly among 4 individual serving plates; top evenly with clam sauce. Sprinkle each serving with Parmesan cheese. Garnish each serving with a fresh basil sprig, if desired. Yield: 4 (1½-cup) servings.

PER SERVING: 237 CALORIES (8% FROM FAT)
FAT 2.1G (SATURATED FAT 0.9G)
PROTEIN 11.1G CARBOHYDRATE 43.5G
CHOLESTEROL 12MG SODIUM 269MG

Linguine with Red Clam Sauce

Chicken Tetrazzini

CHICKEN TETRAZZINI

1 tablespoon margarine
3 cups sliced fresh mushrooms
⅓ cup minced onion
½ cup all-purpose flour
2⅓ cups canned no-salt-added chicken broth, undiluted
2 cups skim milk
¼ cup light process cream cheese product
¼ cup grated Parmesan cheese, divided
¼ cup dry sherry
½ teaspoon salt
½ teaspoon garlic powder
¼ teaspoon pepper
1 (2-ounce) jar diced pimiento, drained
1 (7-ounce) package spaghetti (cooked without salt or fat)
2 cups chopped cooked chicken breast (about ¾ pound skinned, boned chicken breast)
Vegetable cooking spray

Melt margarine in a large saucepan over medium heat; add mushrooms and onion, and sauté 7 minutes or until liquid evaporates. Stir in flour.

Gradually add broth, milk, and cream cheese product; bring to a boil, and cook 5 minutes, stirring constantly. Remove from heat; stir in 2 tablespoons Parmesan cheese and next 5 ingredients.

Stir spaghetti and chicken into mushroom mixture. Spoon mixture into a deep 3-quart casserole coated with cooking spray. Sprinkle with remaining 2 tablespoons Parmesan cheese.

Cover casserole, and bake at 350° for 20 minutes. Bake, uncovered, 10 minutes. Let stand 5 minutes before serving. Yield: 6 (1⅓-cup) servings.

PER SERVING: 371 CALORIES (19% FROM FAT)
FAT 8.0G (SATURATED FAT 3.0G)
PROTEIN 29.9G CARBOHYDRATE 42.3G
CHOLESTEROL 59MG SODIUM 453MG

STRAW AND HAY

1 cup skim milk
½ cup low-fat cottage cheese
1 tablespoon cornstarch
½ cup freshly grated Parmesan cheese, divided
¼ teaspoon salt
⅛ teaspoon freshly ground pepper
⅛ teaspoon ground nutmeg
Vegetable cooking spray
4 ounces diced lean cooked ham
1 clove garlic, crushed
½ cup frozen English peas
4 ounces fettuccine, uncooked
4 ounces spinach fettuccine, uncooked

Combine milk, cottage cheese, and cornstarch in container of an electric blender or food processor. Cover and process until smooth. Transfer milk mixture to a medium-size nonstick skillet. Place over medium heat; add ¼ cup Parmesan cheese, salt, pepper, and nutmeg, stirring until cheese melts. Set aside.

Coat a large nonstick skillet with cooking spray; place over medium heat until hot. Add ham and garlic; sauté 2 minutes. Stir in peas, and sauté 2 minutes. Remove from heat, and stir in milk mixture. Set aside.

Cook fettuccine and spinach fettuccine according to package directions, omitting salt and fat; drain. Place in a large bowl; pour ham mixture over pasta, tossing gently until well combined. Sprinkle with remaining ¼ cup Parmesan cheese. Serve immediately. Yield: 12 (½-cup) servings.

PER SERVING: 118 CALORIES (21% FROM FAT)
FAT 2.7G (SATURATED FAT 1.3G)
PROTEIN 8.7G CARBOHYDRATE 15.2G
CHOLESTEROL 30MG SODIUM 325MG

Straw and Hay

Classic Lasagna

CLASSIC LASAGNA

¾ pound Italian-flavored turkey sausage
1½ cups chopped onion
4 cloves garlic, minced
¼ cup Burgundy or other dry red wine
2 tablespoons red wine vinegar
⅛ teaspoon crushed red pepper
2 (14½-ounce) cans no-salt-added stewed
    tomatoes, undrained and chopped
1 (6-ounce) can no-salt-added tomato paste
¼ cup chopped fresh parsley
⅛ teaspoon pepper
1 (15-ounce) container nonfat ricotta cheese
1 egg white
Vegetable cooking spray
12 cooked lasagna noodles (cooked without
    salt or fat)
1 cup (4 ounces) shredded provolone cheese

Cook turkey sausage in a large saucepan over medium heat until browned, stirring to crumble sausage. Drain; wipe drippings from pan with a paper towel. Return sausage to skillet. Add onion and garlic; sauté 5 minutes. Add Burgundy and next 4 ingredients; stir well. Cover, reduce heat, and simmer 10 minutes. Remove from heat, and set aside.

Combine parsley and next 3 ingredients; stir well, and set aside.

Spread ½ cup tomato mixture in bottom of a 13- x 9- x 2-inch baking dish coated with cooking spray. Arrange 4 noodles over tomato mixture; top noodles with 2 cups tomato mixture, half of the ricotta cheese mixture, and ⅓ cup shredded provolone cheese. Repeat the layers, beginning and ending with noodles. Spread the remaining 1½ cups tomato mixture over noodles, and sprinkle with the remaining ⅓ cup provolone cheese.

Cover and bake at 350° for 20 minutes. Uncover and bake an additional 10 minutes. Let stand 5 minutes before serving. Yield: 9 servings.

PER SERVING: 335 CALORIES (21% FROM FAT)
FAT 8.0G (SATURATED FAT 3.5G)
PROTEIN 23.5G CARBOHYDRATE 44.6G
CHOLESTEROL 37MG SODIUM 373MG

BOLOGNESE SAUCE

2 cups boiling water
1 ounce dried porcini mushrooms
Vegetable cooking spray
1 tablespoon olive oil
1¼ cups chopped onion
¾ cup chopped carrot
½ cup chopped celery
3 cloves garlic, minced
½ pound ground round
½ pound freshly ground raw turkey
½ pound ground veal
½ cup Chablis or other dry white wine
4 (14½-ounce) cans no-salt-added whole
    tomatoes, undrained and chopped
2 bay leaves
½ teaspoon salt
¼ teaspoon freshly ground pepper
½ cup skim milk
1 teaspoon dried whole oregano
1 teaspoon dried whole thyme
⅛ teaspoon ground nutmeg

Pour 2 cups boiling water over mushrooms; let stand 30 minutes. Drain mushrooms through 2 layers of cheesecloth, reserving 1 cup liquid. Coarsely chop mushrooms, and set mushrooms and reserved liquid aside.

Coat a Dutch oven with cooking spray; add oil. Place over medium-high heat until hot. Add onion, carrot, celery, and garlic; sauté until tender. Add ground round, turkey, and veal; cook until meat is browned, stirring until it crumbles. Drain meat mixture, and pat dry with paper towels. Wipe drippings from Dutch oven with a paper towel.

Return meat mixture to Dutch oven; add wine. Bring mixture to a boil, and boil 2 minutes. Add mushrooms and reserved 1 cup liquid, chopped tomato, bay leaves, salt, and pepper. Bring mixture to a boil; cover, reduce heat, and simmer 3 hours, stirring occasionally. Remove and discard bay leaves. Stir in milk, oregano, thyme, and nutmeg. Serve over pasta. Yield: 10 (1-cup) servings.

PER SERVING: 169 CALORIES (24% FROM FAT)
FAT 4.5G (SATURATED FAT 1.2G)
PROTEIN 16.5G CARBOHYDRATE 13.6G
CHOLESTEROL 45MG SODIUM 193MG

Traditional Meat Sauce

TRADITIONAL MEAT SAUCE

6 ounces lean, boneless sirloin steak
6 ounces pork tenderloin
4 ounces lean veal shoulder
Vegetable cooking spray
1 (28-ounce) can plum tomatoes, undrained
1 teaspoon olive oil
⅓ cup finely chopped onion
1 clove garlic, crushed
½ cup water
2 (8-ounce) cans no-salt-added tomato sauce
1 (6-ounce) can tomato paste
1 tablespoon chopped fresh basil
1 teaspoon minced fresh oregano
⅛ teaspoon pepper
1 bay leaf
Fresh basil sprigs (optional)

Trim fat from steak, pork, and veal; slice each diagonally across grain into ⅛-inch strips.

Coat a large Dutch oven with cooking spray, and place over medium-high heat until hot. Add meats; sauté 4 minutes, browning on all sides. Remove steak mixture from pan; drain and pat dry with paper towels, and set aside. Wipe drippings from pan with a paper towel.

Position knife blade in food processor bowl; add tomato. Process until smooth; set aside.

Coat Dutch oven with cooking spray; add olive oil, and place over medium heat until hot. Add onion and garlic; sauté 3 minutes. Add water, stirring to loosen any browned particles from bottom of pan. Return meat mixture to pan. Add pureed tomato, tomato sauce, and next 5 ingredients; stir well. Reduce heat to medium-low. Cook, uncovered, 1 hour or until mixture is reduced to 5⅓ cups; remove bay leaf. Serve sauce over cooked fettuccine. Garnish with fresh basil, if desired. Yield: 8 (⅔-cup) servings.

PER SERVING: 142 CALORIES (22% FROM FAT)
FAT 3.5G (SATURATED FAT 1.0G)
PROTEIN 14.6G CARBOHYDRATE 14.0G
CHOLESTEROL 39MG SODIUM 219MG

EASY TOMATO SAUCE

2 teaspoons olive oil
½ cup finely chopped onion
2 cloves garlic, minced
2 (28-ounce) cans plum tomatoes, undrained and chopped
¼ cup chopped fresh basil
2 teaspoons minced fresh oregano
⅛ to ¼ teaspoon pepper

Heat oil in a large skillet over medium-low heat until hot. Add onion, and sauté until tender. Add garlic; sauté 1 minute. Stir in tomato, and bring to a boil. Add remaining 3 ingredients; stir well. Reduce heat to medium-low, and cook, uncovered, 1 hour and 20 minutes or until thickened, stirring frequently. Serve sauce over cooked pasta. Yield: 8 (½-cup) servings.

PER SERVING: 60 CALORIES (26% FROM FAT)
FAT 1.7G (SATURATED FAT 0.3G)
PROTEIN 2.2G CARBOHYDRATE 10.6G
CHOLESTEROL 0MG SODIUM 324MG

FIERY TOMATO SAUCE

Prepare sauce as directed. Add ¼ teaspoon crushed red pepper with last 3 ingredients. Yield: 8 (½-cup) servings.

PER SERVING: 60 CALORIES (26% FROM FAT)
FAT 1.7G (SATURATED FAT 0.3G)
PROTEIN 2.2G CARBOHYDRATE 10.7G
CHOLESTEROL 0MG SODIUM 324MG

TOMATO AND MUSHROOM SAUCE

Sauté onion and garlic as directed. Add 2 cups chopped fresh mushrooms to sautéed onion mixture. Stir in tomato, and bring to a boil. Add remaining ingredients, and stir well. Reduce heat to medium-low, and cook, uncovered, 1 hour and 30 minutes or until thickened, stirring frequently. Yield: 8 (½-cup) servings.

PER SERVING: 64 CALORIES (25% FROM FAT)
FAT 1.8G (SATURATED FAT 0.3G)
PROTEIN 2.6G CARBOHYDRATE 11.5G
CHOLESTEROL 0MG SODIUM 325MG

MARINARA SAUCE

Vegetable cooking spray
2 teaspoons olive oil
2 cups chopped onion
8 small cloves garlic, minced
8 cups peeled, seeded, and chopped tomato
½ cup chopped fresh parsley
¼ cup minced fresh basil
2 teaspoons minced fresh oregano
1 teaspoon fennel seeds, crushed
½ teaspoon salt
¼ teaspoon pepper

Coat a large saucepan with cooking spray; add oil, and place over medium heat until hot. Add onion and garlic; sauté 3 minutes or until tender. Stir in tomato and remaining ingredients; bring to a boil. Reduce heat, and simmer, uncovered, 30 minutes, stirring occasionally.

Position knife blade in food processor bowl; add 3 cups tomato mixture. Process until smooth. Add tomato puree back to tomato mixture in saucepan; bring to a boil. Reduce heat, and simmer, uncovered, 15 minutes, stirring occasionally. Serve over pasta, fish, or chicken. Yield: 12 (½-cup) servings.

PER SERVING: 47 CALORIES (25% FROM FAT)
FAT 1.3G (SATURATED FAT 0.2G)
PROTEIN 1.6G   CARBOHYDRATE 8.9G
CHOLESTEROL 0MG   SODIUM 111MG

Marinara Sauce

Basil Pesto with Spaghetti

BASIL PESTO WITH SPAGHETTI

4 cloves garlic
2 cups fresh sweet basil, divided
¼ cup no-salt-added chicken broth, undiluted
2 tablespoons water
2 tablespoons olive oil
½ cup grated Parmesan cheese
4 cups hot cooked spaghetti (cooked without salt or fat)

Position knife blade in food processor bowl. With processor running, drop garlic through food chute; process 10 seconds. Add 1 cup basil; pulse until chopped. Add remaining 1 cup basil and next 4 ingredients; pulse until blended. Combine ½ cup basil mixture and spaghetti; toss gently to coat. Reserve remaining pesto for another use. Yield: 8 (½-cup) servings.

Note: Pesto sauce may be stored in an airtight container in the freezer.

PER SERVING: 133 CALORIES (22% FROM FAT)
FAT 3.3G (SATURATED FAT 1.0G)
PROTEIN 5.0G CARBOHYDRATE 20.4G
CHOLESTEROL 3MG SODIUM 69MG

HERE'S THE MEAT!

*B*ack in the eighties somebody's grandma bellowed, "Where's the beef?" and made television history. To that now all-American expression, we answer, "Here's the meat!" for we offer recipes not only containing beef and veal but also pork.

You may be wondering, "Where's the fat?" There's not much here. Red meats naturally high in fat become a healthy ingredient (below the 30 percent fat level) when combined with pasta, which is high in carbohydrates but low in fat.

Dish up hearty recipes such as Ziti Casserole (page 46) and Vermicelli with Sweet-Hot Beef (page 49), and "Where's the pasta?" will become a familiar refrain around the house, especially at dinnertime.

Fettuccine with Vegetables and Ham (Recipe follows on page 52)

Ziti Casserole

½ pound lean ground chuck
½ pound freshly ground raw turkey breast
Vegetable cooking spray
1 cup chopped onion
1 cup sliced fresh mushrooms
¾ cup chopped green pepper
2 cloves garlic, minced
1 cup water
¼ cup chopped fresh parsley
1½ teaspoons dried Italian seasoning
½ teaspoon salt
½ teaspoon pepper
2 (14½-ounce) cans no-salt-added whole
    tomatoes, undrained and chopped
1 (6-ounce) can Italian-style tomato paste
3 cups cooked ziti (short tubular pasta),
    cooked without salt or fat
½ cup freshly grated Parmesan cheese

Cook ground chuck and turkey in a Dutch oven over medium heat until browned, stirring to crumble. Drain and pat dry with paper towels; set aside. Wipe drippings from pan with a paper towel.

Coat pan with cooking spray; place over medium-high heat until hot. Add onion, mushrooms, green pepper, and garlic; sauté 4 minutes or until tender. Return turkey mixture to pan; add water and next 6 ingredients. Bring to a boil; reduce heat, and simmer, uncovered, 25 minutes, stirring occasionally. Remove from heat, and cool slightly.

Add pasta; stir well. Spoon into a 13- x 9- x 2-inch baking dish. Cover with heavy-duty aluminum foil; cut 3 slashes in foil. Bake at 375° for 50 minutes. Uncover; top with cheese. Cover and let stand 5 minutes. Yield: 8 (1⅓-cup) servings.

PER SERVING: 229 CALORIES (25% FROM FAT)
FAT 6.4G (SATURATED FAT 2.8G)
PROTEIN 16.3G   CARBOHYDRATE 27.2G
CHOLESTEROL 31MG   SODIUM 307MG

Hearty Hamburger Stew

Vegetable cooking spray
1 pound ground round
1 cup chopped onion
3 cups water
1 (14½-ounce) can no-salt-added whole
    tomatoes, undrained and chopped
½ cup chopped celery
2 teaspoons beef-flavored bouillon granules
2 teaspoons low-sodium Worcestershire sauce
⅛ teaspoon pepper
1 bay leaf
1 (10-ounce) package frozen baby lima beans
1 (8¾-ounce) can no-salt-added whole kernel
    corn, drained
4 ounces small shell macaroni, uncooked

Coat a Dutch oven with cooking spray; place over medium heat until hot. Add ground round and onion; cook until meat is browned, stirring to crumble. Drain meat mixture; pat dry with paper towels. Wipe drippings from pan with a paper towel.

Return meat mixture to pan; add water and next 6 ingredients, stirring well. Bring to a boil; cover, reduce heat, and simmer 30 minutes.

Add lima beans, corn, and macaroni; bring to a boil. Reduce heat, and simmer, uncovered, 20 minutes, stirring occasionally. Remove and discard bay leaf. Yield: 9 (1-cup) servings.

PER SERVING: 189 CALORIES (17% FROM FAT)
FAT 3.5G (SATURATED FAT 1.1G)
PROTEIN 15.8G   CARBOHYDRATE 22.9G
CHOLESTEROL 31MG   SODIUM 293MG

Did You Know?

In Cincinnati, chili is made with ground beef and flavored with cinnamon. When served over spaghetti, it's called 2-Way. Grated Cheddar cheese ups it to 3-Way. Add chopped onion for 4-Way, and toss in some kidney beans for 5-Way.

4-Way Cincinnati Meat Chili

4-WAY CINCINNATI MEAT CHILI

Vegetable cooking spray
3½ cups chopped onion, divided
1 cup chopped green pepper
2 cloves garlic, minced
1 pound ground round
2 teaspoons ground cinnamon
2 teaspoons paprika
1 teaspoon chili powder
1 teaspoon ground cumin
½ teaspoon ground allspice
½ teaspoon dried whole marjoram
¼ teaspoon ground nutmeg
1 (3-inch) stick cinnamon
¾ teaspoon salt
¼ teaspoon pepper
2 (14½-ounce) cans no-salt-added whole
   tomatoes, undrained and chopped
4½ cups hot cooked spaghetti
¾ cup shredded reduced-fat Cheddar cheese
36 oyster crackers

Coat a large Dutch oven with cooking spray; place over medium-high heat until hot. Add 2 cups onion and next 3 ingredients; cook until meat is browned, stirring to crumble. Add ground cinnamon and next 7 ingredients; cook 1 minute. Add salt, pepper, and tomato; simmer, uncovered, 20 minutes. Discard cinnamon stick.

To serve, arrange ¾ cup spaghetti on each of 6 individual serving plates. Spoon 1 cup chili over spaghetti on each plate, and top with 2 tablespoons cheese and ¼ cup onion. Serve each with 6 crackers. Yield: 6 servings.

Note: See box at left for variations on this dish.

PER SERVING: 392 CALORIES (18% FROM FAT)
FAT 7.7G (SATURATED FAT 3.0G)
PROTEIN 29.7G CARBOHYDRATE 51.5G
CHOLESTEROL 52MG SODIUM 514MG

CHILI-BEEF MACARONI

This hearty supper entrée takes 10 minutes or less
to prepare and only 15 minutes to cook.

3 ounces elbow macaroni, uncooked
¾ pound lean ground chuck
Vegetable cooking spray
½ cup chopped onion
¼ cup chopped green pepper
1 clove garlic, minced
1 tablespoon Dijon mustard
2 teaspoons chili powder
2 teaspoons lemon juice
¾ teaspoon ground cumin
½ teaspoon pepper
¼ teaspoon salt
1 (15-ounce) can dark red kidney beans,
    drained
1 (14½-ounce) can no-salt-added whole
    tomatoes, undrained and chopped
1 (8-ounce) can no-salt-added tomato sauce

Cook macaroni according to package directions, omitting salt and fat. Drain.

Cook meat in a skillet over medium heat until browned, stirring to crumble. Drain; pat dry with paper towels. Wipe drippings from skillet with a paper towel.

Coat skillet with cooking spray; place over medium-high heat until hot. Add onion, green pepper, and garlic; sauté until tender. Add meat, macaroni, mustard, and remaining ingredients; stir well. Bring to a boil. Cover, reduce heat, and simmer 10 minutes, stirring occasionally. Yield: 6 (1-cup) servings.

PER SERVING: 266 CALORIES (30% FROM FAT)
FAT 8.8G (SATURATED FAT 3.2G)
PROTEIN 17.0G CARBOHYDRATE 30.0G
CHOLESTEROL 33MG SODIUM 286MG

MEATY SPAGHETTI

1½ pounds ground chuck
1 medium onion, chopped
1 cup chopped celery
½ cup chopped green pepper
2 cloves garlic, minced
1 (15-ounce) can tomato sauce
1 (6-ounce) can tomato paste
¾ cup water
1 (4-ounce) can mushroom stems and pieces,
    undrained
1½ teaspoons dried whole oregano
½ teaspoon salt
½ teaspoon pepper
1 (12-ounce) package thin spaghetti, uncooked

Cook ground chuck in a Dutch oven over medium heat until meat is browned, stirring to crumble. Drain meat in a colander, and pat dry with paper towels. Wipe drippings from pan with a paper towel.

Return meat to Dutch oven; add onion, celery, green pepper, and garlic. Cook over low heat 5 minutes, stirring frequently. Add tomato sauce and next 6 ingredients, and stir well; bring to a boil. Cover, reduce heat, and simmer 1½ hours, stirring occasionally.

Cook spaghetti according to package directions, omitting salt and fat; drain. Spoon meat sauce over spaghetti. Yield: 8 servings.

PER SERVING: 378 CALORIES (30% FROM FAT)
FAT 12.7G (SATURATED FAT 4.7G)
PROTEIN 22.9G CARBOHYDRATE 43.0G
CHOLESTEROL 50MG SODIUM 591MG

Fat Burner

Take a hike! For fitness, that is. A few times around the block can help you lose weight, burn fat, and decrease your risk of heart disease. Walking can be done almost anywhere or anytime (take a cue from the "mall walkers"), and it requires no equipment except a sturdy pair of shoes. Best of all, it's free and fun.

VERMICELLI WITH SWEET-HOT BEEF

7 ounces vermicelli, uncooked
1 pound ground round
¼ cup raisins
1¼ teaspoons black pepper
1¼ teaspoons ground cumin
½ teaspoon salt
¼ teaspoon ground cinnamon
⅛ teaspoon ground red pepper
½ cup water
1 (8-ounce) can no-salt-added tomato sauce
2 teaspoons lemon juice
Chopped fresh parsley (optional)

Cook vermicelli according to package directions, omitting salt and fat. Drain and set aside.

Cook ground round in a large skillet over medium-high heat until browned, stirring to crumble. Drain and pat dry with paper towels. Wipe drippings from skillet with a paper towel.

Return meat to skillet; add raisins and next 7 ingredients, stirring well. Cook over low heat 15 minutes, stirring occasionally. Stir in lemon juice. Serve over vermicelli. Sprinkle with chopped parsley, if desired. Yield: 5 servings.

PER SERVING: 321 CALORIES (18% FROM FAT)
FAT 6.3G (SATURATED FAT 2.1G)
PROTEIN 25.3G CARBOHYDRATE 39.9G
CHOLESTEROL 56MG SODIUM 293MG

Vermicelli with Sweet-Hot Beef

ORIENTAL NOODLES WITH BEEF AND VEGETABLES

1 (¾-pound) lean flank steak
½ cup plus 2 tablespoons canned low-sodium
   chicken broth, undiluted
1½ tablespoons low-sodium soy sauce
1 tablespoon hoisin sauce
½ teaspoon chili paste
Vegetable cooking spray
2 teaspoons vegetable oil, divided
1 large sweet red pepper, cut into julienne strips
1 large green pepper, cut into julienne strips
1 cup chopped green onions, divided
1 tablespoon minced garlic
1½ cups sliced fresh mushrooms
8 ounces cellophane noodles (cooked without
   salt or fat)

Partially freeze steak; trim fat from steak. Slice
steak diagonally across grain into ⅛-inch-thick
slices; set aside.

Combine chicken broth and next 3 ingredients in
a small bowl; stir well, and set aside.

Coat a wok or large nonstick skillet with cooking
spray; add 1 teaspoon oil. Heat at medium-high
(375°) until hot. Add peppers, and stir-fry 1 minute.
Add ¾ cup green onions and garlic; stir-fry 1
minute. Remove vegetables from wok; keep warm.

Add remaining 1 teaspoon oil to wok; heat at
medium-high until hot. Add steak and mushrooms;
stir-fry 2 minutes. Add cooked noodles, and toss
well. Add chicken broth mixture and vegetable
mixture; stir well. Cook, stirring constantly, 2 to 3
minutes or until mixture is thoroughly heated.
Sprinkle with remaining ¼ cup chopped green
onions. Yield: 7 (1-cup) servings.

PER SERVING: 229 CALORIES (27% FROM FAT)
FAT 6.9G (SATURATED FAT 2.2G)
PROTEIN 11.6G CARBOHYDRATE 29.6G
CHOLESTEROL 24MG SODIUM 223MG

BEEF AND BOW TIE PASTA

9 ounces lean flank steak
⅔ pound fresh green beans, trimmed and cut
   diagonally into 2-inch pieces (about 3 cups)
1 medium-size sweet yellow pepper, cut into
   1-inch pieces (about 1 cup)
¼ cup minced fresh parsley
2 teaspoons dried whole thyme
¼ teaspoon black pepper
Dash of ground red pepper
Vegetable cooking spray
½ cup chopped shallots (about 4)
2 tablespoons dry sherry
2 cups farfalle (bow tie pasta), uncooked
¼ teaspoon salt

Partially freeze flank steak; trim fat from steak.
Slice steak diagonally across grain into ⅛-inch-
thick strips, and set aside.

Arrange green beans in a vegetable steamer over
boiling water. Cover and steam 9 minutes or until
crisp-tender. Add sweet yellow pepper, and steam
2 minutes; remove from heat, and set aside.

Combine parsley and next 3 ingredients in a
medium bowl; stir well. Add steak, tossing gently.
Coat a large nonstick skillet with cooking spray;
place over medium heat until hot. Add steak mixture, shallots, and dry sherry; sauté 3 minutes or to
desired degree of doneness. Drain and wipe drippings from skillet with a paper towel. Return steak
mixture to skillet, and set aside.

Cook pasta according to package directions, omitting salt and fat. Drain well. Add pasta, bean mixture, and salt to steak mixture; toss gently. Serve
warm. Yield: 4 (1½-cup) servings.

PER SERVING: 364 CALORIES (22% FROM FAT)
FAT 8.7G (SATURATED FAT 3.4G)
PROTEIN 21.6G CARBOHYDRATE 49.9G
CHOLESTEROL 35MG SODIUM 202MG

Beef and Bow Tie Pasta

Veal with Peppercorn Sauce

1½ pounds veal cutlets
¼ teaspoon salt
⅛ teaspoon pepper
Vegetable cooking spray
¼ cup chopped onion
¾ cup water
¼ cup Chablis or other dry white wine
1 tablespoon lemon juice
1 teaspoon chicken-flavored bouillon granules
1 teaspoon crushed green peppercorns
½ teaspoon low-sodium Worcestershire sauce
3 cups cooked vermicelli (cooked without salt or fat)
2 teaspoons cornstarch
1 tablespoon water
Fresh parsley sprigs (optional)

Trim fat from veal. Place veal between 2 sheets of heavy-duty plastic wrap, and flatten to ⅛-inch thickness, using a meat mallet or rolling pin. Cut veal into ½-inch strips; sprinkle with salt and pepper. Set aside.

Coat a large nonstick skillet with cooking spray; place over medium-high heat until hot. Add onion; sauté until tender. Add veal strips; cook 2 to 3 minutes on each side or until browned. Add ¾ cup water and next 5 ingredients. Bring to a boil; cover, reduce heat, and simmer 10 minutes.

Place vermicelli on a large platter; arrange veal strips over vermicelli, using a slotted spoon.

Combine cornstarch and 1 tablespoon water, stirring well; add to pan juices. Cook, stirring constantly, until thickened. Spoon sauce over veal strips and vermicelli. Garnish with fresh parsley sprigs, if desired. Yield: 6 servings.

PER SERVING: 235 CALORIES (15% FROM FAT)
FAT 4.0G (SATURATED FAT 1.0G)
PROTEIN 26.4G CARBOHYDRATE 21.6G
CHOLESTEROL 94MG SODIUM 335MG

Fettuccine with Vegetables and Ham

(pictured on page 44)

Small amounts of steamed fresh vegetables can be used if the frozen broccoli, cauliflower, and carrot mix is not available.

8 ounces fettuccine, uncooked
¼ cup water
1 (16-ounce) package frozen broccoli, cauliflower, and carrots
1 cup skim milk
½ cup grated Romano cheese
8 (¾-ounce) slices smoked cured ham, cut into ½-inch squares
½ teaspoon pepper

Cook fettuccine according to package directions, omitting salt and fat; drain. Place in a large bowl, and keep warm.

Bring water to a boil in a medium saucepan. Add vegetables; cook, uncovered, 3 minutes or until vegetables are crisp-tender. Drain; set aside, and keep warm.

Place milk in a small saucepan; cook over low heat until warm. Add warm milk and cheese to fettuccine; stir until thoroughly heated. Stir in reserved vegetables, ham, and pepper. Serve warm. Yield: 7 (1-cup) servings.

PER SERVING: 215 CALORIES (12% FROM FAT)
FAT 2.9G (SATURATED FAT 1.4G)
PROTEIN 13.8G CARBOHYDRATE 35.2G
CHOLESTEROL 15MG SODIUM 435MG

Menu Helper

Don't throw out the leftovers! Cook your favorite pasta, and toss it with cooked vegetables, leftover meat or poultry, and any commercial reduced-calorie dressing or marinade.

Shells with Mushrooms, Ham, and Peas

SHELLS WITH MUSHROOMS, HAM, AND PEAS

1 cup plus 2 tablespoons medium shell
    macaroni, uncooked
1 teaspoon margarine
½ cup chopped onion
1½ cups sliced fresh mushrooms
1 ounce low-sodium 96%-fat-free ham, cut into
    julienne strips
1 tablespoon all-purpose flour
½ cup evaporated skimmed milk
½ cup frozen English peas
2 tablespoons freshly grated Romano cheese

Cook pasta according to package directions, omitting salt and fat. Drain and set aside.

Melt margarine in a saucepan over medium heat;
add onion, and sauté 5 minutes. Add mushrooms
and ham; sauté 2 minutes. Add flour; stir well.
Gradually add milk, and bring to a boil, stirring
constantly.

Reduce heat to medium-low; add peas, and cook
1 minute or until thickened, stirring constantly.
Serve over pasta; sprinkle with Romano cheese.
Yield: 2 servings.

PER SERVING: 314 CALORIES (16% FROM FAT)
FAT 5.6G (SATURATED FAT 1.8G)
PROTEIN 18.0G CARBOHYDRATE 48.3G
CHOLESTEROL 17MG SODIUM 337MG

Pork-and-Asparagus Linguine

1 pound fresh asparagus
1¼ pounds lean, boneless pork loin roast
Vegetable cooking spray
1 tablespoon reduced-calorie margarine
4 cups sliced fresh mushrooms
1 tablespoon plus 1 teaspoon all-purpose flour
1½ cups skim milk
½ cup grated Parmesan cheese, divided
⅛ teaspoon ground nutmeg
⅛ teaspoon pepper
6 cups hot cooked linguine (cooked without salt or fat)

Snap off tough ends of asparagus. Remove scales with a knife or vegetable peeler, if desired. Cut asparagus into 1-inch pieces. Drop asparagus into a saucepan of boiling water, and return to a boil. Cook 3 minutes or until crisp-tender. Drain asparagus; set aside.

Trim fat from roast, and cut into ½-inch pieces. Coat a large saucepan with cooking spray, and place over medium-high heat until hot. Add pork, and cook 7 minutes or until done. Drain well, and set aside.

Melt margarine in saucepan over medium heat. Add mushrooms; sauté 7 minutes or until tender.

Sprinkle mushrooms with flour; stir well, and cook an additional minute. Gradually stir in milk, and cook, stirring constantly, 5 minutes or until thickened. Add asparagus, pork, ¼ cup cheese, nutmeg, and pepper. Stir well.

Serve pork mixture over hot linguine, and sprinkle with remaining ¼ cup cheese. Yield: 6 servings.

PER SERVING: 432 CALORIES (25% FROM FAT)
FAT 12.2G (SATURATED FAT 4.4G)
PROTEIN 30.4G   CARBOHYDRATE 49.7G
CHOLESTEROL 58MG   SODIUM 219MG

Bacon-Broccoli Rigatoni

For variety, substitute 3 ounces smoked or roasted turkey for the Canadian bacon.

4 ounces rigatoni (short tubular pasta), uncooked
Vegetable cooking spray
1 tablespoon plus 1 teaspoon olive oil, divided
3 cups small fresh broccoli flowerets
1⅓ cups (2- x ½-inch) julienne-cut sweet red pepper
½ (6-ounce) package lean Canadian-style bacon, cut into ¼-inch strips
2 cloves garlic, minced

Cook rigatoni according to package directions, omitting salt and fat. Drain rigatoni, and set aside.

Coat a large skillet with vegetable cooking spray; add 1 tablespoon olive oil, and place over medium-high heat until hot. Add broccoli; cook 8 minutes or until very brown, stirring frequently. Remove broccoli from skillet, and set aside.

Add remaining 1 teaspoon oil to skillet, and place over medium-high heat until hot. Add sweet red pepper, and cook 5 minutes or until pepper just begins to blacken. Reduce heat; return broccoli to skillet. Add Canadian bacon and garlic; cook 2 minutes, stirring occasionally.

Combine pasta and broccoli mixture in a bowl; toss well. Yield: 4 (1-cup) servings.

PER SERVING: 209 CALORIES (30% FROM FAT)
FAT 7.0G (SATURATED FAT 1.2G)
PROTEIN 10.4G   CARBOHYDRATE 27.2G
CHOLESTEROL 11MG   SODIUM 321MG

Bacon-Broccoli Rigatoni

PASTA & POULTRY

*W*ant to ensure successful meals? Rely on two basics—chicken and pasta. Their mild flavors complement a variety of seasonings. For Italian flair, try super-easy Chicken Cacciatore Capellini (page 59). Or if you're in the mood for Tex-Mex, go with Mexicali Chicken (page 63). If you crave Oriental dishes but not take-out prices, Chinese Orange Chicken (page 60) is in order.

Don't forget to include turkey in your menu plans. Growing in popularity and availability, low-fat ground turkey takes the place of ground beef in our recipe for Turkey-Noodle Casserole (page 67) and Turkey-Spinach Cannelloni (page 68).

Chunky Chicken Noodle Soup (Recipe follows on page 58)

CHUNKY CHICKEN NOODLE SOUP

(pictured on page 56)

8 (6-ounce) skinned chicken breast halves
1 quart water
3 fresh celery leaves
¾ teaspoon poultry seasoning
¼ teaspoon dried whole thyme
2 cups water
2 cups medium noodles made without egg
    yolks, uncooked
½ cup sliced celery
½ cup sliced carrot
⅓ cup sliced green onions
2 tablespoons minced fresh parsley
1½ teaspoons chicken-flavored bouillon granules
½ teaspoon coarsely ground pepper
1 bay leaf
Coarsely ground pepper

Combine chicken, 1 quart water, celery leaves, poultry seasoning, and thyme in a large Dutch oven; bring to a boil. Cover, reduce heat, and simmer 45 minutes or until chicken is tender.

Remove chicken from broth, reserving broth. Let chicken cool to touch. Bone and coarsely chop chicken; set aside. Skim fat from broth, and strain broth through a double layer of cheesecloth, discarding celery leaves and herbs.

Combine broth, 2 cups water, and next 8 ingredients in pan; bring to a boil. Cover, reduce heat, and simmer 20 minutes, stirring occasionally.

Add chicken; bring to a boil. Reduce heat, and simmer an additional 5 minutes, stirring occasionally. Remove and discard bay leaf. Ladle soup into individual bowls, and sprinkle with pepper. Yield: 12 (1-cup) servings.

PER SERVING: 149 CALORIES (22% FROM FAT)
FAT 3.6G (SATURATED FAT 1.0G)
PROTEIN 26.3G   CARBOHYDRATE 0.9G
CHOLESTEROL 70MG   SODIUM 203MG

CHINESE TURKEY DUMPLINGS

Wonton skins are very thin sheets of dough made from flour, eggs, and salt. Available in some supermarkets and most Oriental specialty food shops, they resemble Italian ravioli.

½ pound freshly ground raw turkey
1 (8-ounce) can sliced water chestnuts,
    drained and finely chopped
⅓ cup finely chopped green onions
¼ cup low-sodium teriyaki sauce, divided
1 egg white, lightly beaten
2 teaspoons peeled, grated gingerroot
40 fresh or frozen wonton skins, thawed
Vegetable cooking spray
⅓ cup dry sherry
1 teaspoon chili oil
½ teaspoon chili powder

Combine first 6 ingredients in a medium bowl; stir well. Place 1 heaping teaspoon turkey mixture in center of each wonton skin. Bring sides of wontons up around filling, and pinch together to form individual bundles.

Arrange bundles in a single layer in a steaming basket coated with cooking spray. Place over boiling water; cover and steam 20 minutes. Transfer dumplings to a serving platter.

Combine sherry, chili oil, and chili powder in a small saucepan; stir well. Bring to a boil; cook 1 minute. Serve with dumplings. Yield: 40 appetizers.

PER APPETIZER: 38 CALORIES (9% FROM FAT)
FAT 0.4G (SATURATED FAT 0.1G)
PROTEIN 2.3G   CARBOHYDRATE 6.0G
CHOLESTEROL 4MG   SODIUM 91MG

CHICKEN CACCIATORE CAPELLINI

6 ounces capellini (angel hair pasta), uncooked
4 (4-ounce) skinned, boned chicken breast
     halves
1¼ cups coarsely chopped onion
1¼ cups coarsely chopped green pepper
2 cups commercial low-fat, low-sodium
     spaghetti sauce
¼ teaspoon salt

Cook pasta according to package directions, omitting salt and fat. Drain pasta, and set aside.

Place a nonstick skillet over medium-high heat until hot. Add chicken, onion, and green pepper. Cook chicken 3 minutes on each side or until lightly browned, stirring vegetables occasionally.

Add spaghetti sauce and salt. Cover, reduce heat, and simmer 15 minutes or until chicken is done. Serve chicken mixture over pasta. Yield: 4 servings.

PER SERVING: 364 CALORIES (8% FROM FAT)
FAT 3.4G (SATURATED FAT 0.9G)
PROTEIN 34.6G CARBOHYDRATE 43.6G
CHOLESTEROL 66MG SODIUM 596MG

Sodium Alert

Many healthy pasta sauces are available at the grocery store for quick pasta fix-ups. Check the nutrient labels to determine which are lower in fat and sodium. If you choose one that is higher in sodium, watch out for sources of additional sodium (such as salt you might add to the pasta's cooking water).

CHICKEN PICCATA

2 (4-ounce) skinned, boned chicken breast
     halves
3 tablespoons all-purpose flour
¼ teaspoon pepper
Vegetable cooking spray
2 tablespoons chopped green onions
3 cloves garlic, minced
1 teaspoon margarine
1 cup hot cooked linguine (cooked without salt
     or fat)
2 tablespoons water
2 tablespoons dry sherry
2 tablespoons lemon juice
1 teaspoon capers

Place each chicken piece between 2 sheets of heavy-duty plastic wrap; flatten to ¼-inch thickness, using a meat mallet or rolling pin. Combine flour and pepper; dredge chicken in flour mixture. Set aside.

Coat a skillet with cooking spray; place over medium heat until hot. Add green onions and garlic; sauté 2 minutes. Remove from pan; set aside.

Add margarine to skillet; place over medium heat until margarine melts. Add chicken; sauté 4 minutes on each side or until done. Arrange chicken and pasta on a serving platter; set aside, and keep warm.

Add green onion mixture, water, and next 3 ingredients to skillet. Cook over high heat 1½ minutes, stirring frequently. Spoon sauce over chicken and pasta. Yield: 2 servings.

PER SERVING: 274 CALORIES (14% FROM FAT)
FAT 4.2G (SATURATED FAT 0.8G)
PROTEIN 30.5G CARBOHYDRATE 27.0G
CHOLESTEROL 66MG SODIUM 212MG

Chinese Orange Chicken

CHINESE ORANGE CHICKEN

1 (11-ounce) can mandarin oranges in light
   syrup, undrained
2 teaspoons cornstarch
1 teaspoon sugar
¼ cup plus 2 tablespoons dry sherry
2 tablespoons low-sodium soy sauce
1 tablespoon rice vinegar
1 pound skinned, boned chicken breasts, cut
   into 1-inch pieces
⅛ teaspoon garlic powder
¾ cup julienne-cut sweet red pepper
¾ cup fresh snow pea pods (about 3 ounces)
¼ cup diagonally sliced green onions
2 cups hot cooked Chinese egg noodles or
   spaghetti (cooked without salt or fat)

Drain mandarin oranges, reserving 1 tablespoon syrup; set oranges aside. Combine 1 tablespoon syrup, cornstarch, and sugar in a 1-cup glass measure; stir well. Add sherry, soy sauce, and vinegar; stir well. Microwave, uncovered, at HIGH 2 to 2½ minutes or until thickened and bubbly, stirring with a wire whisk after every minute. Set aside.

Combine chicken and garlic powder in a 2-quart casserole. Cover with wax paper, and microwave at HIGH 4 to 5 minutes or until chicken is done, stirring every 2 minutes. Drain well. Wipe drippings from dish with a paper towel.

Place sweet red pepper in dish; microwave at HIGH 1 minute. Return chicken mixture to dish; add sherry mixture, snow peas, and green onions, stirring well.

Microwave at HIGH 2 to 3 minutes or until thoroughly heated, stirring after every minute. Stir in oranges. Serve over noodles. Yield: 4 servings.

Note: For stir-fry directions, see next page.

PER SERVING: 321 CALORIES (10% FROM FAT)
FAT 3.6G (SATURATED FAT 0.9G)
PROTEIN 30.6G CARBOHYDRATE 38.6G
CHOLESTEROL 72MG SODIUM 268MG

STIR-FRY ORANGE CHICKEN

Chicken and vegetables may be cooked in a non-stick wok, if desired. Coat wok with cooking spray; heat at medium-high (375°) until hot. Drizzle 1 teaspoon vegetable oil around top of wok. Add chicken, and stir-fry 2 minutes or until lightly browned; remove from wok, and set aside.

Add sweet red pepper to wok, and stir-fry 2 minutes; add snow peas and green onions, and stir-fry 1 minute or until vegetables are crisp-tender. Stir in sherry mixture and garlic powder; cook until thoroughly heated. Stir in oranges. Serve over noodles.

CHICKEN FETTUCCINE

Olive oil-flavored vegetable cooking spray
1 pound skinned, boned chicken breast, cut into bite-size pieces
½ cup chopped onion
¼ teaspoon dried whole basil
¼ teaspoon garlic powder
⅛ teaspoon salt
⅛ teaspoon pepper
1 clove garlic, minced
2 cups sliced zucchini
4 cups hot cooked fettuccine (cooked without salt or fat)
¾ cup evaporated skimmed milk
2 tablespoons grated Parmesan cheese

Coat a Dutch oven with cooking spray; place over medium heat until hot. Add chicken and next 6 ingredients; sauté 4 minutes or until chicken loses its pink color. Add zucchini; sauté until tender. Remove from heat; add fettuccine and milk, tossing gently. Sprinkle mixture with cheese before serving. Yield: 4 (1½-cup) servings.

PER SERVING: 394 CALORIES (9% FROM FAT)
FAT 3.8G (SATURATED FAT 1.3G)
PROTEIN 38.8G   CARBOHYDRATE 49.0G
CHOLESTEROL 70MG   SODIUM 265MG

CHICKEN-PEPPER GNOCCHI

Vegetable cooking spray
1½ cups chopped sweet red pepper
½ cup chopped green pepper
1 cup chopped onion
3 cloves garlic, minced
¼ teaspoon ground cumin
¼ teaspoon crushed red pepper
¼ teaspoon salt
1 tablespoon all-purpose flour
1 teaspoon chicken-flavored bouillon granules
½ cup water
½ (16-ounce) package gnocchi or shell pasta, uncooked
4 (4-ounce) skinned, boned chicken breast halves, cut into bite-size pieces
1 (6-ounce) package frozen snow pea pods

Coat a large nonstick skillet with cooking spray; place over medium-high heat until hot. Add sweet red pepper and next 5 ingredients, and sauté until tender. Stir in salt, flour, and bouillon granules. Gradually add water; bring to a boil, stirring constantly. Remove from heat, and pour into container of an electric blender or food processor; cover and process until smooth. Set aside, and keep warm.

Cook gnocchi according to package directions, omitting salt and fat. Drain and set aside.

Coat skillet with cooking spray; place over medium heat until hot. Add chicken; sauté until browned. Add snow peas; cover and cook 1 to 2 minutes. Add chicken and pepper mixtures to gnocchi; toss gently. Yield: 6 servings.

PER SERVING: 215 CALORIES (9% FROM FAT)
FAT 2.1G (SATURATED FAT 0.4G)
PROTEIN 22.6G   CARBOHYDRATE 26.3G
CHOLESTEROL 44MG   SODIUM 295MG

Chicken-Peanut Pasta

CHICKEN-PEANUT PASTA

Purchase fresh spicy-flavored gingerroot with a smooth skin. Peel it before mincing the inside flesh unless the gingerroot is very tender.

2 teaspoons sugar
1½ teaspoons cornstarch
2 teaspoons peeled, minced gingerroot
½ cup water
3 tablespoons low-sodium soy sauce
1½ teaspoons white vinegar
⅛ teaspoon hot sauce
4 cloves garlic, minced
1 pound skinned, boned chicken breast, cut into thin strips
1 teaspoon vegetable oil
1 cup minced green onions
1½ cups fresh snow pea pods, halved
4 cups hot cooked fusilli (corkscrew pasta), cooked without salt or fat
1 teaspoon dark sesame oil
1 teaspoon low-sodium soy sauce
⅓ cup unsalted dry-roasted peanuts

Combine first 8 ingredients in a large bowl; stir well. Add chicken, and toss gently to coat. Cover and chill 1 hour.

Remove chicken from marinade, reserving marinade. Heat vegetable oil in a large skillet over medium-high heat. Add chicken; stir-fry 5 minutes. Add reserved marinade, green onions, and snow peas; stir-fry 2 minutes or until slightly thickened. Remove from heat.

Combine fusilli, sesame oil, and 1 teaspoon soy sauce in a large bowl; toss gently to coat. Add chicken mixture and peanuts, tossing gently. Yield: 6 (1¼-cup) servings.

PER SERVING: 305 CALORIES (21% FROM FAT)
FAT 7.1G (SATURATED FAT 1.2G)
PROTEIN 25.7G CARBOHYDRATE 34.2G
CHOLESTEROL 44MG SODIUM 325MG

MEXICALI CHICKEN

⅓ cup chopped green onions
¼ cup chopped green pepper
1 teaspoon minced garlic
¾ teaspoon pepper
1 (14½-ounce) can no-salt-added whole tomatoes, undrained and chopped
1 (4-ounce) can chopped green chiles, drained
1 cup canned low-sodium chicken broth, undiluted
1 tablespoon fresh lemon juice
4 ounces wagon wheel pasta, uncooked
2 cups chopped cooked chicken
¼ cup chopped fresh cilantro
3 tablespoons sliced ripe olives

Combine first 8 ingredients in a large skillet. Cook, uncovered, over medium-high heat 20 minutes. Cook pasta according to package directions, omitting salt and fat; drain. Add pasta, chicken, cilantro, and olives to tomato mixture. Cover, reduce heat, and simmer 20 minutes. Yield: 5 servings.

PER SERVING: 258 CALORIES (23% FROM FAT)
FAT 6.6G (SATURATED FAT 1.6G)
PROTEIN 24.4G CARBOHYDRATE 25.0G
CHOLESTEROL 61MG SODIUM 240MG

Menu Helper

Don't limit pasta to the usual Italian flavors. Give it a Mexican accent by combining your favorite commercial salsa with pasta and cooked black beans or black-eyed peas.

SPINACH AND CHICKEN MOSTACCIOLI CASSEROLE

*Resembling "little mustaches,"
mostaccioli is the name given to 2-inch-long
tubes of pasta cut on the diagonal.*

10 ounces mostaccioli (tubular pasta),
       uncooked
1 (10-ounce) package frozen chopped spinach,
     thawed
Vegetable cooking spray
2 teaspoons vegetable oil
⅔ cup chopped onion
2 large cloves garlic, minced
1 pound skinned, boned chicken breast, cut
     into 1-inch pieces
2 (14½-ounce) cans no-salt-added whole
     tomatoes, undrained and coarsely chopped
3 tablespoons no-salt-added tomato paste
1¼ teaspoons dried whole basil
¾ teaspoon dried whole oregano
¼ teaspoon salt
¼ teaspoon crushed red pepper
½ cup grated Parmesan cheese, divided

Cook mostaccioli according to package directions, omitting salt and fat; drain and set aside. Place spinach on paper towels; squeeze until barely moist. Set spinach aside.

Coat a large nonstick skillet with cooking spray; add oil, and place over medium-high heat until hot. Add onion and garlic; sauté until tender. Add chicken; cook, stirring constantly, just until chicken loses its pink color. Stir in tomato and next 5 ingredients; bring to a boil. Reduce heat, and simmer, uncovered, 5 minutes, stirring occasionally.

Combine pasta, spinach, chicken mixture, and ¼ cup Parmesan cheese in a bowl; stir well. Spoon into a 13- x 9- x 2-inch baking dish coated with cooking spray. Sprinkle with remaining ¼ cup cheese. Bake at 350° for 20 minutes. Yield: 8 (1½-cup) servings.

PER SERVING: 277 CALORIES (16% FROM FAT)
FAT 4.8G (SATURATED FAT 1.9G)
PROTEIN 22.9G   CARBOHYDRATE 35.5G
CHOLESTEROL 38MG   SODIUM 287MG

JALAPEÑO CHICKEN AND PASTA

Olive oil-flavored vegetable cooking spray
3 (4-ounce) skinned, boned chicken breast
     halves, cut into 1-inch cubes
2 medium-size sweet red peppers, seeded and
     cut into 1-inch pieces
2 medium-size sweet yellow peppers, seeded
     and cut into 1-inch pieces
10 ounces fresh shiitake mushrooms, sliced
2 cloves garlic, minced
1 jalapeño pepper, seeded and chopped
3 tablespoons Chablis or other dry white wine
½ cup canned low-sodium chicken broth,
     undiluted
6 ounces rigatoni (short tubular pasta),
     uncooked
1 tablespoon olive oil
¼ cup diagonally sliced green onions
¼ cup freshly grated Parmesan cheese
¼ teaspoon salt
⅛ teaspoon freshly ground pepper
¼ cup chopped fresh cilantro

Coat a large nonstick skillet with cooking spray; place over medium-high heat until hot. Add chicken and next 5 ingredients; sauté 4 minutes or until chicken is lightly browned. Add wine, and sauté 2 minutes or until wine evaporates. Add chicken broth; reduce heat to medium, and simmer, uncovered, 2 minutes. Remove chicken mixture from heat, and set aside.

Cook rigatoni according to package directions, omitting salt and fat. Drain well. Place rigatoni in a large bowl; add olive oil, and toss well. Add chicken mixture, and stir well. Add sliced green onions, Parmesan cheese, salt, pepper, and chopped cilantro, tossing gently to combine. Yield: 6 servings.

PER SERVING: 243 CALORIES (20% FROM FAT)
FAT 5.3G (SATURATED FAT 1.4G)
PROTEIN 20.2G   CARBOHYDRATE 27.4G
CHOLESTEROL 36MG   SODIUM 225MG

Jalapeño Chicken and Pasta

CHICKEN ROLLUPS

Vegetable cooking spray
1 cup chopped onion
1 clove garlic, minced
1 (15-ounce) can no-added-salt tomato sauce
1 (6-ounce) can no-added-salt tomato paste
½ cup sliced fresh mushrooms
2 tablespoons chopped fresh parsley
2 tablespoons Burgundy or other dry red wine
1 teaspoon dried whole oregano
¼ teaspoon pepper
1 (12-ounce) carton low-fat cottage cheese
1 egg
½ cup (2 ounces) shredded mozzarella cheese
2 tablespoons grated Parmesan cheese
2 cups finely chopped cooked chicken breast
8 cooked lasagna noodles (cooked without salt
    or fat)
2 tablespoons grated Parmesan cheese

Coat a large skillet with cooking spray; place over medium heat until hot. Add onion and garlic; sauté until tender. Add tomato sauce and next 6 ingredients, and bring to a boil. Cover; reduce heat, and simmer 30 minutes, stirring occasionally.

Combine cottage cheese and next four ingredients, stirring well. Chill thoroughly.

Spread 1 cup tomato sauce mixture in bottom of a 13- x 9- x 2-inch baking dish coated with cooking spray. Stir chicken into remaining tomato sauce mixture, and set aside.

Spread ¼ cup cottage cheese mixture on each lasagna noodle. Spread 2 tablespoons chicken mixture over cheese on each noodle; roll up jellyroll fashion, beginning at narrow end. Arrange lasagna rolls, seam side down, in prepared dish. Spoon remaining chicken mixture over rolls; sprinkle with 2 tablespoons Parmesan cheese. Cover and bake at 350° for 30 to 40 minutes. Yield: 8 servings.

PER SERVING 296 CALORIES (18% FROM FAT)
FAT 6.0G (SATURATED FAT 2.8G)
PROTEIN 26.1G CARBOHYDRATE 33.6G
CHOLESTEROL 70MG SODIUM 325MG

CHICKEN LASAGNA

1 tablespoon plus 1 teaspoon margarine, divided
1½ pounds skinned, boned chicken breast, cut
    into bite-size pieces
4 cloves garlic, crushed and divided
6 cups sliced fresh mushrooms (about 1 pound)
6 cups thinly sliced leek
3 tablespoons all-purpose flour
2½ cups 2% low-fat milk
1½ cups freshly grated Parmesan cheese, divided
1 cup nonfat ricotta cheese
½ teaspoon dried whole basil
¼ teaspoon salt
¼ teaspoon pepper
12 lasagna noodles, uncooked
Vegetable cooking spray
5 cups coarsely shredded zucchini (1¼ pounds)

Melt 1 teaspoon margarine in a large skillet over medium heat. Add chicken and 2 cloves garlic; sauté 4 minutes or until chicken is done. Remove from skillet; set aside. Add remaining 2 cloves garlic and mushrooms to skillet; sauté 10 minutes or until liquid evaporates. Set aside.

Melt remaining 1 tablespoon margarine in a large saucepan over medium heat; add leek. Cover and cook 30 minutes, stirring occasionally. Sprinkle with flour, stirring until well blended. Gradually add milk, stirring with a wire whisk. Cook over medium heat, stirring constantly, 8 minutes or until thickened. Stir in chicken mixture, ½ cup Parmesan cheese, ricotta cheese, and seasonings.

Arrange 4 uncooked noodles in bottom of a 13- x 9- x 2-inch baking dish coated with cooking spray. Top with half of zucchini, ⅓ cup Parmesan cheese, half of mushroom mixture, and 2 cups chicken mixture. Repeat layers, beginning and ending with uncooked noodles. Spread the remaining 2 cups chicken mixture over noodles; sprinkle with remaining ⅓ cup Parmesan cheese. Cover and chill 8 hours. Bake, covered, at 350° for 1 hour. Uncover and bake 15 minutes. Let stand 5 minutes before serving. Yield: 9 servings.

PER SERVING: 427 CALORIES (19% FROM FAT)
FAT 9.1G (SATURATED FAT 4.1G)
PROTEIN 36.8G CARBOHYDRATE 50.3G
CHOLESTEROL 62MG SODIUM 385MG

CHICKEN SPAGHETTI

1 pound chicken breast halves, skinned
5 cups water
3 ounces spaghetti, uncooked
1 tablespoon margarine
1 tablespoon all-purpose flour
2 tablespoons skim milk
⅛ teaspoon pepper
Vegetable cooking spray
⅓ cup chopped onion
¼ cup chopped celery
¼ cup chopped green pepper
1 clove garlic, minced
1 (14½-ounce) can no-salt-added stewed
  tomatoes, undrained
⅛ teaspoon crushed red pepper
¼ cup (1 ounce) shredded Cheddar cheese

Place chicken in a small Dutch oven; add water, and bring to a boil. Cover; reduce heat, and simmer 20 minutes or until chicken is tender. Remove chicken from broth; let cool. Set aside ½ cup broth; reserve remaining broth for other uses. Bone chicken, and cut meat into bite-size pieces; set aside.

Cook spaghetti according to package directions, omitting salt and fat; drain well, and set aside.

Melt margarine in a small saucepan; add flour, stirring until smooth. Cook 1 minute, stirring constantly. Gradually stir in skim milk and ½ cup reserved chicken broth. Cook over medium heat, stirring constantly, until thickened and bubbly. Stir in ⅛ teaspoon pepper. Remove milk mixture from heat, and set aside.

Coat a large skillet with cooking spray, and place over medium heat until hot. Add onion, celery, green pepper, and garlic; sauté until tender. Stir in tomato, red pepper, and milk mixture. Stir in spaghetti and chicken.

Spoon into a 1½-quart casserole coated with cooking spray. Cover and bake at 350° for 20 minutes. Uncover and sprinkle with shredded cheese; bake an additional 5 minutes or until cheese melts. Yield: 4 servings.

PER SERVING: 304 CALORIES (25% FROM FAT)
FAT 8.5G (SATURATED FAT 2.8G)
PROTEIN 28.7G CARBOHYDRATE 27.2G
CHOLESTEROL 68MG SODIUM 171MG

TURKEY-NOODLE CASSEROLE

(pictured on page 2)

Vegetable cooking spray
1 pound freshly ground raw turkey
½ cup sliced fresh mushrooms
¼ cup chopped onion
2 (8-ounce) cans no-salt-added tomato sauce
¼ teaspoon garlic powder
¼ teaspoon pepper
¼ teaspoon dried whole oregano
⅛ teaspoon salt
1 cup nonfat ricotta cheese
3 tablespoons skim milk
½ (8-ounce) package Neufchâtel cheese, softened and cut into ½-inch cubes
2 teaspoons poppy seeds
6 ounces wide egg noodles (cooked without salt
  or fat)
Fresh parsley sprig

Coat a large nonstick skillet with cooking spray; place over medium-high heat until hot. Add turkey, mushrooms, and onion; cook until turkey is browned and onion is tender, stirring to crumble. Drain and pat turkey mixture dry with paper towels. Wipe drippings from skillet with a paper towel.

Return turkey mixture to skillet. Add tomato sauce and next 4 ingredients. Bring to a boil; reduce heat, and simmer, uncovered, 3 minutes, stirring occasionally.

Combine ricotta cheese and milk in container of an electric blender; cover and process until smooth. Transfer to a bowl; stir in Neufchâtel cheese and poppy seeds. Add noodles; toss to coat.

Place two-thirds of noodle mixture in an 11- x 7- x 2-inch baking dish. Spread turkey mixture over noodle mixture, leaving a 1-inch border. Top with remaining one-third of noodle mixture, leaving a 1-inch border of the turkey mixture. Cover and bake at 400° for 20 to 25 minutes or until thoroughly heated. Garnish with parsley. Yield: 6 servings.

PER SERVING: 321 CALORIES (26% FROM FAT)
FAT 9.1G (SATURATED FAT 4.0G)
PROTEIN 29.3G CARBOHYDRATE 31.1G
CHOLESTEROL 89MG SODIUM 211MG

TURKEY-SPINACH CANNELLONI

12 cannelloni shells, uncooked
3 cups canned no-salt-added tomato sauce
¼ teaspoon dried whole oregano
¼ teaspoon dried whole basil
¼ teaspoon salt
2 cloves garlic, minced
Olive oil-flavored vegetable cooking spray
½ cup chopped onion
1 teaspoon minced garlic
1 pound freshly ground raw turkey
1 (10-ounce) package frozen chopped spinach,
    thawed and drained
½ cup 1% low-fat cottage cheese
2 tablespoons nonfat sour cream alternative
½ cup frozen egg substitute, thawed
½ teaspoon dried whole oregano
¼ cup reduced-calorie margarine
¼ cup all-purpose flour
1¾ cups skim milk
¼ teaspoon salt
⅛ teaspoon ground white pepper
⅓ cup (1⅓ ounces) shredded part-skim
    mozzarella cheese
1 tablespoon freshly grated Parmesan cheese

Cook cannelloni shells according to package directions, omitting salt and fat; drain and set aside.

Combine tomato sauce and next 4 ingredients; spread 1 cup sauce in a 13- x 9- x 2-inch baking dish coated with cooking spray. Set aside remaining sauce.

Coat a large skillet with cooking spray. Place over medium-high heat until hot; add onion and 1 teaspoon minced garlic. Sauté until onion is tender. Add turkey; cook over medium heat until turkey is done, stirring to crumble. Drain turkey mixture.

Combine turkey mixture, spinach, and next 4 ingredients. Fill cannelloni shells with turkey mixture, and place over tomato sauce in baking dish; set aside.

Melt margarine in a medium-size saucepan over medium heat; add flour, stirring until blended. Cook 1 minute, stirring constantly. Gradually add skim milk; cook over medium heat, stirring constantly, until mixture is thickened. Add salt and pepper; stir sauce well. Pour white sauce over stuffed cannelloni.

Spoon remaining tomato sauce mixture over white sauce. Sprinkle with cheeses. Cover and bake at 375° for 30 minutes. Uncover and bake 5 additional minutes or until thoroughly heated and bubbly. Yield: 6 servings.

PER SERVING: 448 CALORIES (21% FROM FAT)
FAT 10.6G (SATURATED FAT 2.8G)
PROTEIN 34.0G   CARBOHYDRATE 53.0G
CHOLESTEROL 51MG   SODIUM 558MG

Spread 1 cup tomato sauce mixture in the baking dish before adding the stuffed cannelloni so the bottoms of the shells will stay soft.

Using a teaspoon, carefully fill the cooked cannelloni shells with the turkey mixture, being careful not to tear shells.

Sprinkle mozzarella cheese and freshly grated Parmesan cheese over the shells and tomato sauce before baking.

Turkey-Spinach Cannelloni

SEAFOOD SAMPLER

Cook a little pasta, toss in some crabmeat or shrimp, add a salad or vegetable side dish, and dinner is done. The health benefits of pasta have been touted for years. Seafood has its own attributes, providing plenty of protein but little saturated fat. And although not officially classified as seafood, catfish and salmon offer the same healthy advantages when paired with pasta. These tasty recipes (page 72) are followed by a medley of seafood dishes, with ingredients ranging from clams to shrimp.

You can prepare many of these pasta-seafood combos quickly—check out the Colorful Crabmeat and Linguine (page 78) or Scallop and Pasta Toss (page 82). If you've got more time, try Seafood Lasagna Florentine (page 84). It takes a little longer, but the results are worth the effort.

Shrimp and Asparagus Medley (Recipe follows on page 83)

CATFISH PASTA PRIMAVERA

1 pound farm-raised catfish fillets, cut into
   cubes
2 cups hot cooked linguine (cooked without
   salt or fat)
1 teaspoon vegetable oil
Vegetable cooking spray
1 cup snow pea pods, trimmed
½ cup broccoli flowerets
⅓ cup thinly sliced yellow squash
½ cup (2-inch pieces) green onions
1 small sweet red pepper, seeded and cut into
   strips
1 clove garlic, minced
1 cup skim milk
2 teaspoons cornstarch
¼ cup plus 2 tablespoons grated Parmesan
   cheese
2 tablespoons plus 2 teaspoons minced fresh
   parsley
¼ teaspoon white pepper
2 tablespoons dry sherry
1 teaspoon reduced-calorie margarine
1 teaspoon lime juice

Rinse fillets under cold running water; pat dry,
and set aside.

Toss linguine and oil in a large bowl; set aside,
and keep warm.

Coat a large skillet with cooking spray; place over
medium heat until hot. Add catfish, and sauté 5 minutes or until fish flakes easily when tested with a
fork. Remove from skillet; set aside, and keep warm.

Add snow peas and next 5 ingredients to skillet;
sauté 3 minutes or until the vegetables are crisp-
tender. Remove from skillet, and set aside.

Combine milk and cornstarch in skillet; stir until
smooth. Add catfish, vegetables, cheese, and next 5
ingredients; cook over medium heat until heated,
stirring constantly. Pour over hot linguine; toss
gently. Yield: 4 (1½-cup) servings.

PER SERVING: 352 CALORIES (27% FROM FAT)
FAT 10.7G (SATURATED FAT 3.6G)
PROTEIN 32.3G   CARBOHYDRATE 30.5G
CHOLESTEROL 75MG   SODIUM 319MG

FETTUCCINE ALFREDO WITH SALMON

*Spinach pasta makes an attractive dish, but plain
fettuccine will work just as well.*

1 (1-pound) salmon fillet
Vegetable cooking spray
⅛ teaspoon freshly ground pepper
2 tablespoons reduced-calorie margarine
3 cloves garlic, minced
2 tablespoons all-purpose flour
2 cups skim milk
¾ cup grated fresh Parmesan cheese, divided
6 cups hot cooked spinach fettuccine (cooked
   without salt or fat)

Place salmon, skin side down, on a broiler rack
coated with cooking spray; place rack on a broiler
pan. Sprinkle salmon with pepper. Broil 5½ inches
from heat (with electric oven door partially opened)
11 minutes or until salmon flakes easily when tested with a fork. Flake salmon into bite-size pieces;
set aside, and keep warm.

Melt margarine in a medium saucepan over
medium heat; add garlic, and sauté 1 minute. Add
flour; cook 1 minute, stirring constantly with a wire
whisk. Gradually add milk, stirring constantly.
Cook an additional 8 minutes or until slightly
thickened and bubbly, stirring constantly. Add ½
cup plus 2 tablespoons cheese; stir until cheese
melts. Pour over pasta, and toss well. Top with
salmon; sprinkle with remaining 2 tablespoons
cheese. Yield: 6 servings.

PER SERVING: 427 CALORIES (27% FROM FAT)
FAT 12.9G (SATURATED FAT 3.6G)
PROTEIN 29.5G   CARBOHYDRATE 46.5G
CHOLESTEROL 59MG   SODIUM 305MG

Fettuccine Alfredo with Salmon

MINESTRONE WITH CLAMS

1 cup dried baby lima beans
1 tablespoon olive oil
2 cups finely chopped onion
1 teaspoon fennel seeds, crushed
1 teaspoon dried whole thyme
3 cloves garlic, minced
5 (10½-ounce) cans low-sodium chicken broth
2 cups diced zucchini
1 cup small shell macaroni, uncooked
½ cup chopped fresh flat-leaf parsley
¾ teaspoon grated lemon rind
¼ teaspoon salt
¼ teaspoon crushed red pepper
1 (10-ounce) can whole baby clams, undrained
¼ cup plus 1 tablespoon grated Parmesan
   cheese
Fresh steamed clams (optional)

Sort and wash beans; place in a large Dutch oven. Cover with water 2 inches above beans, and bring to a boil; cook 2 minutes. Remove from heat; cover and let stand 1 hour. Drain beans.

Heat oil in pan over medium heat. Add onion and next 3 ingredients; sauté 5 minutes. Add beans and broth; bring to a boil. Cover, reduce heat, and simmer 1 hour. Add zucchini and next 6 ingredients; cook 15 minutes or until pasta is done. Ladle soup into individual soup bowls; sprinkle with Parmesan cheese. Garnish with fresh clams, if desired. Yield: 10 (1-cup) servings.

PER SERVING: 138 CALORIES (24% FROM FAT)
FAT 3.7G (SATURATED FAT 0.8G)
PROTEIN 8.2G CARBOHYDRATE 18.4G
CHOLESTEROL 11MG SODIUM 323MG

Minestrone with Clams

CAPELLINI WITH CLAM SAUCE

Vegetable cooking spray
1 teaspoon olive oil
⅓ cup chopped onion
2 tablespoons chopped green pepper
2 cloves garlic, minced
3 cups unpeeled, seeded, and chopped tomato
1 (8-ounce) can no-salt-added tomato sauce
½ teaspoon crushed red pepper
¼ teaspoon salt
1 (6½-ounce) can minced clams
¼ cup chopped fresh flat-leaf parsley
8 ounces capellini (angel hair pasta), uncooked

Coat a large nonstick skillet with cooking spray; add oil. Place over medium-high heat until hot. Add onion, green pepper, and garlic; sauté until tender. Stir in tomato and next 3 ingredients. Cover, reduce heat, and simmer 20 minutes.

Drain clams; reserve juice. Add juice to tomato mixture, and simmer an additional 5 minutes. Stir in clams and parsley; cook 5 minutes or until thoroughly heated. Remove from heat; keep warm.

Cook pasta according to package directions, omitting salt and fat; drain. Place pasta in a large bowl. Add clam mixture, and toss gently. Serve immediately. Yield: 5 (1-cup) servings.

PER SERVING: 242 CALORIES (9% FROM FAT)
FAT 2.4G (SATURATED FAT 0.4G)
PROTEIN 10.4G CARBOHYDRATE 45.0G
CHOLESTEROL 12MG SODIUM 353MG

ANGEL HAIR PASTA WITH CRABMEAT AND ASIAGO

Asiago is a rich-flavored, hard Italian cheese. Parmesan is a suitable substitute.

Vegetable cooking spray
2 cups sliced fresh mushrooms
½ cup sliced green onions
¾ pound fresh lump crabmeat, drained
¾ cup seedless green grapes
¾ cup seedless red grapes
½ cup Chablis or other dry white wine
3 tablespoons chopped fresh basil
3 tablespoons chopped fresh flat-leaf parsley
4 cups hot cooked capellini (angel hair pasta), cooked without salt or fat
¾ cup (3 ounces) grated Asiago or Parmesan cheese

Coat a large skillet with cooking spray; place over medium heat until hot. Add mushrooms and green onions, and sauté 4 minutes or until tender. Add crabmeat, green and red grapes, and wine; cook 7 minutes or until most of liquid evaporates. Add basil and parsley; cook 30 seconds. Arrange 1 cup pasta on each of 4 serving plates; top each serving with 1 cup crabmeat mixture and 3 tablespoons Asiago cheese. Yield: 4 servings.

PER SERVING: 416 CALORIES (18% FROM FAT)
FAT 8.5G (SATURATED FAT 3.9G)
PROTEIN 32.9G CARBOHYDRATE 51.9G
CHOLESTEROL 99MG SODIUM 585MG

Did You Know?

Many cooks use imitation crabmeat, made from surimi, instead of the much more expensive "real" crabmeat. Surimi is a fish product made from inexpensive whitefish to imitate the flavor, texture, and shape of various types of seafood such as crabmeat, shrimp, lobster, and scallops.

Surimi is rich in protein, low in cholesterol and fat, and fully cooked and ready to eat when purchased. Still, it is not the perfect substitute for fresh seafood, especially if you are watching your sodium intake; surimi's sodium content is often higher than that of fresh seafood.

Crabmeat and Pasta Casserole

CRABMEAT AND PASTA CASSEROLE

1 cup fusilli (corkscrew pasta), uncooked
½ pound fresh asparagus
Vegetable cooking spray
1 tablespoon plus 1 teaspoon reduced-calorie
    margarine, divided
2 small carrots, scraped and cut into julienne
    strips
½ medium-size green pepper, seeded and
    chopped
1 green onion, cut diagonally into ½-inch
    pieces
3 tablespoons Chablis or other dry white wine
1½ tablespoons all-purpose flour
1½ cups skim milk
1½ tablespoons grated Parmesan cheese
1 teaspoon chicken-flavored bouillon granules
½ pound fresh lump crabmeat or imitation
    crabmeat, drained

Cook fusilli according to package directions, omitting salt and fat. Drain; set aside.

Snap off tough ends of asparagus. Remove scales from stalks with a knife or vegetable peeler, if desired. Cut asparagus into 1½-inch pieces.

Coat a large heavy skillet with cooking spray; add 1 teaspoon margarine, and place over medium-high heat until margarine melts. Add asparagus, carrot, green pepper, and green onion; sauté 2 to 3 minutes or until crisp-tender. Add wine, and cook, uncovered, over medium heat until liquid evaporates. Remove vegetables from skillet, and set aside.

Add remaining 1 tablespoon margarine to skillet; place over low heat until margarine melts. Add flour, stirring until smooth. Cook, stirring constantly, 1 minute. Gradually add skim milk, and cook over medium heat, stirring constantly with a wire whisk, until mixture thickens. Add Parmesan cheese and bouillon granules, stirring well.

Coat an 11- x 7- x 1½-inch baking dish with cooking spray. Combine fusilli, vegetables, cheese sauce, and crabmeat; stir well. Spoon into baking dish. Cover and bake at 350° for 20 to 25 minutes or until thoroughly heated. Serve immediately. Yield: 4 servings.

PER SERVING: 237 CALORIES (19% FROM FAT)
FAT 5.1G (SATURATED FAT 0.9G)
PROTEIN 20.0G   CARBOHYDRATE 28.0G
CHOLESTEROL 60MG   SODIUM 494MG

CHINESE CURLY NOODLES WITH CRABMEAT

Vegetable cooking spray
1 teaspoon dark sesame oil
⅓ pound fresh snow pea pods, trimmed
1 (7-ounce) package crimini or other fresh
    mushrooms, sliced
1 cup canned low-sodium chicken broth,
    undiluted
1 tablespoon low-sodium soy sauce
2 teaspoons minced garlic
1 teaspoon peeled, minced gingerroot
2 cups shredded fresh spinach
1 pound fresh lump crabmeat, drained
8 ounces Chinese curly noodles or angel hair
    pasta, uncooked

Coat a large nonstick skillet with cooking spray; add oil. Place over medium-high heat until hot. Add snow peas and mushrooms; sauté 2 minutes. Add chicken broth, soy sauce, garlic, and gingerroot; sauté 1 minute. Add spinach and crabmeat; sauté 3 minutes. Remove from heat, and keep warm.

Cook noodles according to package directions, omitting salt and fat; drain. Place noodles in a serving bowl, and add crabmeat mixture; toss well. Serve immediately. Yield: 8 (1-cup) servings.

PER SERVING: 206 CALORIES (12% FROM FAT)
FAT 2.8G (SATURATED FAT 0.3G)
PROTEIN 17.5G   CARBOHYDRATE 24.8G
CHOLESTEROL 57MG   SODIUM 247MG

CRABMEAT RAVIOLI

Olive oil-flavored vegetable cooking spray
2 teaspoons olive oil, divided
1¼ cups finely chopped fresh mushrooms
¼ cup minced green onions
6 ounces fresh lump crabmeat, drained
2 tablespoons chopped fresh parsley
2½ ounces goat cheese, softened
2 ounces Neufchâtel cheese, softened
2 tablespoons water
1 teaspoon minced fresh thyme
48 fresh or frozen wonton skins, thawed
3 quarts water
3 cups finely chopped tomato
1½ teaspoons minced garlic
1 tablespoon chopped fresh parsley (optional)
Fresh thyme sprigs (optional)

Coat a large nonstick skillet with cooking spray;
add 1 teaspoon olive oil. Place over medium-high
heat until hot. Add mushrooms and green onions;
sauté 1 minute. Add crabmeat, and cook 1 minute.
Stir in 2 tablespoons parsley, cheeses, 2 tablespoons
water, and minced thyme. Reduce heat to low;
cook until cheeses melt, stirring frequently.
Remove from heat; let cool slightly.

Place 1 tablespoon cheese mixture in center of
each of 24 wonton skins. Brush edges of wonton
skins with water; top with remaining 24 wonton
skins. Press wonton edges together to seal, pushing
out air. Trim wonton edges with scissors.

Bring 3 quarts water to a boil in a Dutch oven.
Add one-third of ravioli; return water to a boil.
Reduce heat; simmer, uncovered, 4 minutes or
until ravioli are tender. Remove with a slotted
spoon. Set aside, and keep warm. Repeat procedure with remaining ravioli.

Coat a large nonstick skillet with cooking spray;
add remaining 1 teaspoon oil. Place over medium-
high heat until hot. Add tomato and garlic; stir well.
Reduce heat, and cook, uncovered, 10 minutes.

Position knife blade in food processor bowl; add
tomato mixture. Pulse 5 times or until mixture is
almost smooth.

Place 4 ravioli on each of 6 serving plates. Top
evenly with tomato mixture. Garnish with 1 tablespoon parsley and thyme sprigs, if desired. Serve
immediately. Yield: 6 servings.

PER SERVING: 312 CALORIES (24% FROM FAT)
FAT 8.2G (SATURATED FAT 3.6G)
PROTEIN 16.4G   CARBOHYDRATE 43.0G
CHOLESTEROL 47MG   SODIUM 537MG

COLORFUL CRABMEAT AND LINGUINE

*Round out this simple, yet elegant one-dish meal
with a spinach salad, French bread, and a glass
of sparkling mineral water.*

8 ounces linguine, uncooked
½ pound fresh mushrooms, sliced
½ cup chopped green onions
½ cup chopped sweet red pepper
⅓ cup cream sherry
1 pound fresh lump crabmeat, drained
¼ cup chopped fresh parsley
2 teaspoons lemon juice

Cook linguine according to package directions,
omitting salt and fat. Drain well; set aside, and
keep warm.

Combine mushrooms, green onions, sweet red
pepper, and sherry in a large skillet. Cook over
medium heat, stirring frequently, until vegetables
are tender. Stir in crabmeat, parsley, and lemon
juice; cook until heated.

Place hot linguine evenly on 4 serving plates,
and top evenly with crabmeat mixture. Yield: 4
servings.

PER SERVING: 347 CALORIES (8% FROM FAT)
FAT 3.1G (SATURATED FAT 0.4G)
PROTEIN 30.4G   CARBOHYDRATE 48.1G
CHOLESTEROL 106MG   SODIUM 309MG

Capellini with Lobster

CAPELLINI WITH LOBSTER

2 (8-ounce) fresh or frozen lobster tails, thawed
Butter-flavored vegetable cooking spray
¼ cup minced green onions
2 teaspoons minced garlic
½ cup Chablis or other dry white wine
½ teaspoon ground green peppercorns
¼ cup all-purpose flour
1½ cups skim milk
¾ cup (3 ounces) shredded reduced-fat
    Monterey Jack cheese
2 tablespoons freshly grated Parmesan cheese
6 ounces capellini (angel hair pasta), uncooked
¼ cup chopped fresh flat-leaf parsley
Lemon slices (optional)
Green peppercorns (optional)

Cook lobster tails in boiling water 6 to 8 minutes or until done; drain. Rinse with cold water. Split and clean tails. Reserve shells for garnish, if desired. Coarsely chop lobster meat, and set aside.

Coat a nonstick skillet with cooking spray; place over medium-high heat until hot. Add green onions and garlic; sauté 1 minute or until tender. Add wine and ground peppercorns; cook 2 minutes or until wine evaporates.

Combine flour and milk, stirring until smooth. Add to green onion mixture in skillet; cook over medium heat, stirring constantly with a wire whisk, until thickened and bubbly. Add lobster and cheeses; cook, stirring constantly, 2 minutes or until cheeses melt and lobster is heated.

Cook pasta according to package directions, omitting salt and fat; drain. Combine pasta and lobster mixture in a serving bowl; toss gently. Spoon evenly onto 5 serving plates, and sprinkle with parsley. Garnish with lobster tails, lemon slices, and green peppercorns, if desired. Serve immediately. Yield: 5 (1-cup) servings.

PER SERVING: 299 CALORIES (16% FROM FAT)
FAT 5.2G (SATURATED FAT 2.6G)
PROTEIN 25.5G   CARBOHYDRATE 36.2G
CHOLESTEROL 55MG   SODIUM 414MG

Linguine with Mussels and Red Sauce

LINGUINE WITH MUSSELS AND RED SAUCE

1½ pounds fresh mussels, scrubbed and
     debearded (about 42 mussels)
2 tablespoons cornmeal
1 tablespoon olive oil
½ cup finely chopped onion
1 clove garlic, minced
1 cup Chablis or other dry white wine
1 tablespoon dried whole basil
½ teaspoon crushed red pepper
2 (16-ounce) cans plum tomatoes with basil,
     undrained and chopped
2 (8-ounce) cans no-salt-added tomato sauce
9 cups hot cooked linguine (about 1 pound
     uncooked), cooked without salt or fat
¼ cup chopped fresh parsley

Discard any open mussels; place remaining mussels in a large bowl. Cover with cold water. Sprinkle with cornmeal; let stand 30 minutes. Drain and rinse mussels; set aside. Discard cornmeal.

Heat oil in a large Dutch oven over medium-low heat until hot. Add onion and garlic; cook 5 minutes, stirring frequently. Add wine; bring to a boil over medium heat, and cook 5 minutes. Add basil and next 3 ingredients; reduce heat, and simmer, uncovered, 10 minutes.

Spread mussels, hinged side down, on top of tomato mixture. Cover and cook over high heat 3 minutes or until mussels open; discard any unopened mussel shells.

Spoon ¾ cup linguine into each of 12 large soup bowls; top each with ½ cup sauce, 3 mussels, and 1 teaspoon parsley. Yield: 12 servings.

PER SERVING: 246 CALORIES (12% FROM FAT)
FAT 3.3G (SATURATED FAT 0.5G)
PROTEIN 13.2G   CARBOHYDRATE 40.5G
CHOLESTEROL 16MG   SODIUM 298MG

ANGEL HAIR PASTA WITH SEA SCALLOPS

½ cup soft breadcrumbs
8 ounces capellini (angel hair pasta), uncooked
1 tablespoon plus 1 teaspoon olive oil, divided
½ cup chopped fresh parsley, divided
1 clove garlic, minced
1 teaspoon dried whole basil
½ teaspoon dried whole oregano
¼ teaspoon salt
1 tablespoon all-purpose flour
¼ teaspoon pepper
1 (8-ounce) bottle clam juice
1 pound fresh sea scallops, cut into ½-inch
     pieces

Place breadcrumbs on a baking sheet. Bake at 375° for 5 minutes or until golden brown; set aside.

Cook pasta according to package directions, omitting salt and fat. Drain and rinse under cold running water; drain well. Place in a large bowl; set aside.

Heat 1 tablespoon oil in a nonstick skillet over medium heat. Add ¼ cup parsley and next 4 ingredients; sauté 1 minute. Add flour and pepper; cook 1 minute, stirring constantly with a wire whisk. Gradually add clam juice, stirring constantly. Cook 1 minute or until thickened, stirring constantly. Pour over pasta; toss well. Set pasta mixture aside, and keep warm.

Heat remaining 1 teaspoon oil in skillet over medium heat; add scallops, and sauté 4 minutes or until scallops are done. Add to pasta mixture; toss gently. Sprinkle with toasted breadcrumbs and remaining ¼ cup parsley. Serve immediately. Yield: 4 (1¼-cup) servings.

PER SERVING: 379 CALORIES (16% FROM FAT)
FAT 6.6G (SATURATED FAT 0.9G)
PROTEIN 27.5G   CARBOHYDRATE 50.5G
CHOLESTEROL 38MG   SODIUM 342MG

SCALLOP AND PASTA TOSS

Vegetable cooking spray
1 tablespoon reduced-calorie margarine
2 cups diagonally sliced celery
1 cup sliced fresh mushrooms
½ cup sliced green onions
½ cup sliced carrot
2 cloves garlic, minced
¾ pound fresh bay scallops
2 tablespoons water
2 teaspoons white wine Worcestershire sauce
½ teaspoon ground ginger
¼ teaspoon salt
⅛ teaspoon pepper
4 cups cooked spinach linguine (cooked
    without salt or fat)

Coat a large nonstick skillet with cooking spray; add margarine. Place over medium-high heat until margarine melts. Add celery, mushrooms, green onions, carrot, and garlic; sauté until crisp-tender.

Add scallops and next 5 ingredients to skillet; cook 5 to 7 minutes or until scallops are opaque, stirring occasionally.

Place linguine in a large serving bowl; add scallop mixture, and toss gently. Yield: 4 servings.

PER SERVING: 320 CALORIES (14% FROM FAT)
FAT 4.9G (SATURATED FAT 0.7G)
PROTEIN 23.1G   CARBOHYDRATE 46.2G
CHOLESTEROL 28MG   SODIUM 440MG

Scallop and Pasta Toss

ZESTY SHRIMP AND TORTELLINI

9 ounces fresh spinach tortellini with cheese, uncooked
Vegetable cooking spray
½ cup chopped green pepper
½ cup chopped onion
2 tablespoons chopped fresh parsley
2 cloves garlic, minced
1 (14½-ounce) can no-salt-added whole tomatoes, undrained
1 (6-ounce) can tomato paste
2 tablespoons Burgundy or other dry red wine
1 teaspoon sugar
½ teaspoon dried whole oregano
½ teaspoon dried whole basil
⅛ teaspoon pepper
1 pound medium-size fresh shrimp, peeled and deveined

Cook tortellini according to package directions, omitting salt and fat. Drain and set aside.

Coat a large saucepan with cooking spray; place over medium heat until hot. Add green pepper, onion, parsley, and garlic. Sauté until tender, and set aside.

Place tomato in container of an electric blender; cover and process until smooth. Add to onion mixture; stir in tomato paste and next 5 ingredients. Bring mixture to a boil; cover, reduce heat, and simmer 20 minutes.

Add shrimp to tomato mixture; cook, uncovered, stirring constantly, 3 to 4 minutes or until shrimp turn pink. Stir in tortellini; cook over low heat until thoroughly heated. Yield: 6 servings.

PER SERVING: 258 CALORIES (13% FROM FAT)
FAT 3.8G (SATURATED FAT 1.3G)
PROTEIN 24.4G CARBOHYDRATE 32.2G
CHOLESTEROL 135MG SODIUM 297MG

SHRIMP AND ASPARAGUS MEDLEY

(pictured on page 70)

1 pound fresh asparagus
6 ounces linguine, uncooked
6 cups water
1¾ pounds medium-size fresh shrimp, peeled and deveined
Vegetable cooking spray
1 teaspoon margarine
⅔ cup chopped onion
½ cup diced green pepper
½ pound sliced fresh mushrooms
1 teaspoon dried whole thyme
¼ teaspoon pepper
⅛ teaspoon salt
⅛ teaspoon celery seeds
2 tablespoons lemon juice

Snap off tough ends of asparagus. Remove scales from stalks with a knife or vegetable peeler, if desired. Cut asparagus into 1-inch pieces; set aside.

Cook pasta according to package directions, omitting salt and fat. Drain pasta well. Set pasta aside, and keep warm.

Bring water to a boil in a large saucepan; add shrimp, and cook 3 to 5 minutes or until shrimp turn pink. Drain well, and set aside.

Coat a large nonstick skillet with cooking spray; add margarine. Place over medium-high heat until margarine melts. Add asparagus, onion, and green pepper; sauté until vegetables are crisp-tender.

Add sliced mushrooms, thyme, pepper, salt, and celery seeds; stir well. Cook, uncovered, over medium heat 3 to 4 minutes or until mushrooms are tender, stirring frequently. Stir in shrimp and lemon juice; cook until thoroughly heated, stirring frequently.

Place pasta on a large serving platter; spoon shrimp mixture over pasta. Serve immediately. Yield: 6 servings.

PER SERVING: 225 CALORIES (9% FROM FAT)
FAT 2.3G (SATURATED FAT 0.5G)
PROTEIN 22.3G CARBOHYDRATE 29.3G
CHOLESTEROL 147MG SODIUM 232MG

SEAFOOD LASAGNA FLORENTINE

2 (10-ounce) packages frozen chopped spinach,
    thawed and drained
½ cup all-purpose flour
2 cups 2% low-fat milk
¼ teaspoon salt
¼ teaspoon ground nutmeg
⅛ teaspoon ground red pepper
⅛ teaspoon ground black pepper
1 large clove garlic, crushed
¼ cup Chablis or other dry white wine
⅔ cup grated Parmesan cheese, divided
1 pound fresh bay scallops
½ cup chopped fresh basil
1 tablespoon lemon juice
½ pound fresh lump crabmeat, drained
1 egg, lightly beaten
9 cooked lasagna noodles (cooked without salt
    or fat)
½ teaspoon paprika

Press spinach between paper towels until barely moist; set aside.

Place flour in a shallow baking pan. Bake at 350° for 30 minutes or until lightly browned, stirring after 15 minutes. Spoon flour into a large saucepan; gradually add milk, blending with a wire whisk. Stir in salt and next 4 ingredients; cook over medium heat 5 minutes or until thickened, stirring constantly.

Add wine to milk mixture; cook an additional minute, stirring constantly. Remove from heat; stir in ½ cup Parmesan cheese and scallops. Let cool slightly; stir in basil and next 3 ingredients.

Spoon ¼ cup seafood sauce into a 13- x 9- x 2-inch baking dish. Arrange 3 lasagna noodles in a single layer over seafood sauce, and top with one-third spinach; spoon one-third of remaining seafood sauce over spinach. Repeat layers twice, ending with seafood sauce.

Combine remaining 2 tablespoons plus 2 teaspoons

Seafood Lasagna Florentine

Parmesan cheese and paprika; stir well. Sprinkle cheese mixture over lasagna. Cover and bake at 400° for 30 minutes. Bake, uncovered, an additional 10 minutes. Let stand 10 minutes before serving. Yield: 9 servings.

PER SERVING: 286 CALORIES (16% FROM FAT)
FAT 5.1G (SATURATED FAT 2.2G)
PROTEIN 24.8G   CARBOHYDRATE 33.6G
CHOLESTEROL 75MG   SODIUM 411MG

SOUTHWESTERN SEAFOOD LASAGNA

1 teaspoon margarine
1 cup chopped onion
2 cloves garlic, minced
¼ cup all-purpose flour
¾ cup 1% low-fat milk
1 (8-ounce) bottle clam juice
½ cup sliced green onions
2 tablespoons minced jalapeño pepper
1 (16½-ounce) can no-salt-added cream-style corn
1¼ cups (5 ounces) shredded Monterey Jack cheese
1 cup nonfat ricotta cheese
½ cup light process cream cheese product
¼ cup fresh lime juice
1 pound medium-size fresh unpeeled shrimp
½ pound fresh lump crabmeat, drained
9 cooked lasagna noodles (cooked without salt or fat)
½ teaspoon ground cumin
¼ teaspoon pepper
Vegetable cooking spray

Melt margarine in a saucepan over medium heat. Add chopped onion and garlic; sauté 5 minutes. Place flour in a bowl; gradually add milk, stirring with a wire whisk until blended. Add milk mixture and clam juice to pan; cook 5 minutes or until thickened and bubbly, stirring constantly. Add green onions, jalapeño pepper, and corn. Cook corn mixture 2 minutes, and set aside.

Position knife blade in food processor bowl; add Monterey Jack cheese and next 3 ingredients, and process until smooth.

Peel, devein, and coarsely chop shrimp. Combine shrimp and crabmeat in a bowl; toss gently.

Spread ¾ cup corn mixture in bottom of a 13- x 9- x 2-inch baking dish. Arrange 3 lasagna noodles over corn mixture; top with half of the cheese mixture, half of the shrimp mixture, and ¾ cup corn mixture. Repeat layers, beginning and ending with noodles. Spread remaining corn mixture over noodles, and sprinkle with cumin and pepper.

Cover with aluminum foil coated on the bottom with cooking spray; cut 10 (1-inch) slits in foil. Bake at 375° for 45 minutes. Let stand 5 minutes. Yield: 9 servings.

PER SERVING: 351 CALORIES (24% FROM FAT)
FAT 9.4G (SATURATED FAT 4.8G)
PROTEIN 27.6G   CARBOHYDRATE 40.4G
CHOLESTEROL 106MG   SODIUM 369MG

Quick Tip

Many pasta recipes can be made in stages. Prepare the filling, sauce, and pasta in advance. Then assemble and bake the dish right before mealtime. Or complete the dish ahead of time, and reheat just before serving.

If the pasta is to be baked or cooked further, undercook it slightly in boiling water so that it won't be too soft in the finished dish.

VEGETABLE MEDLEY

*T*here's always one in every family: "I'm tired of vegetables." No problem. When you have a finicky eater, use this "healthy stealth" strategy. Tuck the vegetables between layers of cheese and lasagna noodles, or stuff them inside giant macaroni shells. Pasta makes a wonderful main dish with everything from asparagus to zucchini.

Here the portions are hearty enough to be a main dish, but you can also serve these recipes on the side. Just decrease the portion size. But be prepared—the family may ask for second helpings.

Spinach Fettuccine Toss (Recipe follows on page 90)

Pasta-Vegetable Soup

PASTA-VEGETABLE SOUP

4 cups canned no-salt-added chicken broth,
      undiluted
3 cups water
1 cup sun-dried tomatoes (without salt or oil)
6 ounces farfalle (bow tie pasta), uncooked
4 green onions, sliced
1 tablespoon balsamic vinegar
1 clove garlic, minced
1 (10-ounce) package frozen leaf spinach,
      thawed and drained

Combine first 3 ingredients in a Dutch oven.
Bring to a boil; cover, reduce heat, and simmer 10
minutes or until tomato is soft. Remove tomato
from mixture. Let cool slightly; cut into thin strips.
   Return tomato to pan. Stir in pasta, green onions,
vinegar, and garlic. Bring to a boil; cover, reduce
heat, and simmer 15 minutes or until pasta is tender. Stir in spinach, and cook just until soup is thoroughly heated. Yield: 6 (1½-cup) servings.

PER SERVING: 166 CALORIES (11% FROM FAT)
FAT 2.1G (SATURATED FAT 0.1G)
PROTEIN 7.9G CARBOHYDRATE 29.7G
CHOLESTEROL 0MG SODIUM 321MG

QUICK MINESTRONE SOUP

2 cups diced zucchini
½ cup ditalini (small tubular pasta), uncooked
⅛ teaspoon pepper
2 cloves garlic, minced
2 (16-ounce) cans low-sodium chicken broth
1 (16-ounce) can red kidney beans, drained
1 (14½-ounce) can Italian-style stewed
      tomatoes, undrained and coarsely chopped
1 (10-ounce) package frozen peas and carrots,
      thawed
½ cup grated Parmesan cheese

Combine first 8 ingredients in a large saucepan;
bring to a boil. Cover, reduce heat, and simmer 10
minutes or until pasta is done, stirring occasionally.

Stir in cheese; ladle soup into 6 individual bowls.
Yield: 6 (1½-cup) servings.

PER SERVING: 234 CALORIES (15% FROM FAT)
FAT 3.8G (SATURATED FAT 1.4G)
PROTEIN 13.3G CARBOHYDRATE 38.3G
CHOLESTEROL 5MG SODIUM 412MG

FETTUCCINE-SPINACH SOUP

*Combine this easy soup with breadsticks and
low-fat cheese to boost the protein.*

1 medium carrot, scraped and cut into julienne
      strips
1 medium-size sweet red pepper, seeded and
      cut into julienne strips
3 (13¾-ounce) cans no-salt-added chicken
      broth
1¼ cups water
½ teaspoon dried whole basil
½ teaspoon dried whole oregano
¼ teaspoon salt
2 cups thinly sliced fresh mushrooms
4 ounces fettuccine, uncooked and broken in
      half
1 (10-ounce) package frozen leaf spinach,
      thawed and drained
2 tablespoons plus 2 teaspoons grated
      Parmesan cheese

Combine first 7 ingredients in a Dutch oven.
Bring to a boil; cover, reduce heat, and simmer 5
minutes or until vegetables are tender. Add mushrooms and fettuccine; simmer 10 minutes or until
fettuccine is tender. Remove from heat; stir in
spinach. Ladle soup into individual bowls, and
sprinkle each serving with 1 teaspoon Parmesan
cheese. Yield: 8 (1¼-cup) servings.

PER SERVING: 107 CALORIES (21% FROM FAT)
FAT 2.5G (SATURATED FAT 0.6G)
PROTEIN 5.9G CARBOHYDRATE 14.9G
CHOLESTEROL 2MG SODIUM 249MG

CAPELLINI WITH CILANTRO PESTO

1½ cups firmly packed fresh cilantro
1½ cups firmly packed fresh flat-leaf parsley
2 tablespoons water
1½ tablespoons fresh lime juice
1 tablespoon olive oil
¼ teaspoon salt
3 cloves garlic, halved
8 ounces capellini (angel hair pasta), uncooked
½ cup freshly grated Romano cheese
3 tablespoons chopped walnuts, lightly toasted

Position knife blade in food processor bowl; add first 7 ingredients. Process until smooth, scraping sides of processor bowl occasionally.

Cook pasta according to package directions, omitting salt and fat; drain. Place pasta in a serving bowl. Add cilantro mixture, Romano cheese, and walnuts; toss gently. Serve immediately. Yield: 4 (1-cup) servings.

PER SERVING: 337 CALORIES (29% FROM FAT)
FAT 11.0G (SATURATED FAT 3.2G)
PROTEIN 13.7G CARBOHYDRATE 46.1G
CHOLESTEROL 15MG SODIUM 334MG

Protein Power

You can get plenty of high-quality protein in your pasta meals without meat. How? The different types of protein in pasta and other grains, vegetables, and seeds complement one another when eaten together. The result: two incomplete proteins make a complete protein equivalent to that of meat. Serve protein-powered pasta with legumes, such as dried beans and peanuts. If a meatless dish includes cheese or milk, don't be concerned about the amount of protein. Like meat, dairy foods are complete proteins.

SPINACH FETTUCCINE TOSS

(pictured on page 86)

A salad plus fruit for dessert will make a complete meal. Or offer smaller portions as a side dish with chicken or roast beef.

2 ounces fettuccine, uncooked
2 ounces spinach fettuccine, uncooked
1¼ cups 1% low-fat cottage cheese
¼ cup skim milk
1 teaspoon Dijon mustard
½ teaspoon prepared horseradish
Vegetable cooking spray
1¼ cups chopped sweet red pepper
½ cup sliced green onions
3 tablespoons grated Parmesan cheese
2 tablespoons chopped fresh parsley

Cook fettuccine and spinach fettuccine according to package directions, omitting salt and fat. Drain well, and keep warm.

Combine cottage cheese and next 3 ingredients in container of an electric blender; cover and process until smooth.

Coat a large nonstick skillet with cooking spray; place over medium heat until hot. Add sweet red pepper and green onions; sauté until tender. Add fettuccine, cottage cheese mixture, Parmesan cheese, and parsley; toss gently. Transfer to a serving bowl. Serve warm. Yield: 4 (1-cup) servings.

PER SERVING: 186 CALORIES (13% FROM FAT)
FAT 2.6G (SATURATED FAT 1.2G)
PROTEIN 15.6G CARBOHYDRATE 26.4G
CHOLESTEROL 6MG SODIUM 408MG

GORGONZOLA PASTA

8 ounces radiatore (short, fat rippled pasta), uncooked
1 cup part-skim ricotta cheese
½ cup water
1½ cups frozen English peas, thawed
¼ teaspoon ground red pepper
¼ cup chopped fresh parsley
2 ounces Gorgonzola cheese, crumbled
1 tablespoon chopped walnuts, toasted

Cook pasta according to package directions, omitting salt and fat. Drain and set aside.

Combine ricotta cheese and water in container of an electric blender; cover and process until smooth. Transfer mixture to a small saucepan. Stir in peas and red pepper; cook until thoroughly heated, stirring constantly.

Place pasta in a serving bowl. Add ricotta mixture and parsley; toss gently. Sprinkle with Gorgonzola cheese and walnuts. Serve immediately. Yield: 6 (1-cup) servings.

PER SERVING: 270 CALORIES (24% FROM FAT)
FAT 7.2G (SATURATED FAT 3.9G)
PROTEIN 13.9G CARBOHYDRATE 36.0G
CHOLESTEROL 20MG SODIUM 232MG

CHEESY MANICOTTI

½ cup grated Parmesan cheese, divided
2 cups 1% low-fat cottage cheese
½ cup part-skim ricotta cheese
2 tablespoons chopped fresh parsley
½ teaspoon dried Italian seasoning
¼ teaspoon garlic powder
1 egg, lightly beaten
12 cooked manicotti shells (cooked without salt or fat)
1 (29-ounce) jar no-salt-added spaghetti sauce

Combine ⅓ cup Parmesan cheese and next 6 ingredients in a bowl; stir well. Stuff each shell with ¼ cup cheese mixture; arrange in a 13- x 9- x 2-inch baking dish.

Pour spaghetti sauce over shells. Cover and bake at 375° for 25 minutes or until thoroughly heated. Uncover and sprinkle with remaining Parmesan cheese, and bake an additional 5 minutes. Yield: 6 servings.

PER SERVING: 381 CALORIES (22% FROM FAT)
FAT 9.5G (SATURATED FAT 4.5G)
PROTEIN 23.5G CARBOHYDRATE 52.1G
CHOLESTEROL 51MG SODIUM 506MG

BLUE CHEESE LASAGNA

Vegetable cooking spray
4 cups chopped onion
2 cloves garlic, minced
2 pounds fresh mushrooms, thinly sliced
4 (14½-ounce) cans no-salt-added whole tomatoes, undrained and chopped
1 (8-ounce) can no-salt-added tomato sauce
1 (6-ounce) can tomato paste
2 tablespoons dried Italian seasoning
¼ teaspoon salt
¼ teaspoon pepper
1½ cups (6 ounces) crumbled blue cheese
12 lasagna noodles (cooked without salt or fat)

Coat a large Dutch oven with cooking spray; place over medium heat until hot. Add onion and garlic, and sauté 3 minutes. Add mushrooms, and cook 7 minutes or until tender. Add tomato and next 5 ingredients, and cook 1 hour and 20 minutes or until mixture is reduced to 2 quarts, stirring frequently. Remove from heat; stir in cheese.

Coat a 13- x 9- x 2-inch baking dish with cooking spray. Spoon 1 cup tomato mixture into dish. Arrange 3 cooked lasagna noodles lengthwise over tomato mixture; top with 1¾ cups tomato mixture. Repeat layers 3 times, ending with tomato mixture. Cover and bake at 350° for 20 minutes. Bake, uncovered, an additional 10 minutes. Let stand 5 minutes before serving. Yield: 9 servings.

PER SERVING: 292 CALORIES (21% FROM FAT)
FAT 6.8G (SATURATED FAT 3.7G)
PROTEIN 13.3G CARBOHYDRATE 47.8G
CHOLESTEROL 14MG SODIUM 379MG

PASTA WITH ROASTED PEPPERS AND BASIL

(pictured on cover)

1 tablespoon olive oil
2 cups chopped onion
½ teaspoon fennel seeds, crushed
2 cloves garlic, minced
2 (14½-ounce) cans no-salt-added whole
   tomatoes, undrained and chopped
1 pound green peppers, roasted and peeled
   (about 2 large)
1 pound sweet red peppers, roasted and peeled
   (about 2 large)
1 pound sweet yellow peppers, roasted and
   peeled (about 2 large)
½ teaspoon salt
¼ teaspoon freshly ground pepper
6½ cups cooked penne (short tubular pasta),
   cooked without salt or fat
½ cup thinly sliced fresh basil
½ cup freshly grated Parmesan cheese

Heat oil in a large nonstick skillet over medium-low heat. Add onion, fennel seeds, and garlic; cover and cook 10 minutes or until tender, stirring occasionally. Add tomato, and bring to a boil. Reduce heat, and simmer, uncovered, 30 minutes, stirring occasionally.

Cut roasted peppers into julienne strips. Add pepper strips, salt, and pepper to tomato mixture; cook 3 minutes or until thoroughly heated. Combine tomato mixture, pasta, and basil in a large bowl; toss well. Sprinkle with Parmesan cheese. Yield: 7 (1½-cup) servings.

Note: See instructions for roasting peppers in first paragraph of Colorful Pasta Medley.

PER SERVING: 308 CALORIES (17% FROM FAT)
FAT 5.7G (SATURATED FAT 1.8G)
PROTEIN 11.9G CARBOHYDRATE 54.0G
CHOLESTEROL 6MG SODIUM 320MG

COLORFUL PASTA MEDLEY

1 large sweet red pepper
1 large sweet yellow pepper
1 large green pepper
¾ pound fresh asparagus
Vegetable cooking spray
2 cloves garlic, minced
1 tablespoon lemon juice
¾ cup part-skim ricotta cheese
¾ cup plain nonfat yogurt
6 ounces penne (short tubular pasta), uncooked
¼ cup freshly grated Parmesan cheese
2 tablespoons pine nuts, toasted

Cut peppers in half lengthwise; remove and discard seeds and membrane. Place peppers, skin side up, on an ungreased baking sheet; flatten peppers with palm of hand. Broil 5½ inches from heat (with electric oven door partially opened) 15 to 20 minutes or until peppers blister and turn dark. Place in ice water for 5 minutes; peel. Cut into julienne strips, and set aside.

Snap off tough ends of asparagus. Remove scales with a knife or vegetable peeler, if desired. Cut asparagus into 1-inch pieces. Cook asparagus in a small amount of boiling water 2 to 3 minutes or until crisp-tender. Drain well, and set aside.

Coat a large nonstick skillet with cooking spray; place over medium-high heat until hot. Add pepper strips and garlic; sauté 2 minutes. Add asparagus; sauté 1 minute. Stir in lemon juice. Remove from heat, and set aside.

Combine ricotta cheese and yogurt in container of an electric blender or food processor; cover and process until smooth. Add to pepper mixture.

Cook pasta according to package directions, omitting salt and fat. Drain. Add pasta to ricotta cheese mixture, and toss well to combine. Transfer to a large serving bowl; sprinkle with Parmesan cheese and pine nuts. Yield: 6 (1-cup) servings.

PER SERVING: 236 CALORIES (26% FROM FAT)
FAT 6.7G (SATURATED FAT 3.0G)
PROTEIN 13.6G CARBOHYDRATE 31.9G
CHOLESTEROL 14MG SODIUM 161MG

Colorful Pasta Medley

ASPARAGUS LASAGNA

2 pounds fresh asparagus
3 cups peeled, chopped tomato
2 tablespoons chopped fresh basil
Olive oil-flavored vegetable cooking spray
1 teaspoon olive oil
¼ cup chopped fresh parsley
1 tablespoon minced garlic
¼ cup canned low-sodium chicken broth,
    undiluted
1 (15-ounce) carton part-skim ricotta cheese
½ (8-ounce) container nonfat cream cheese
    product, softened
2 tablespoons lemon juice
¼ cup grated Romano cheese
⅛ teaspoon ground nutmeg
6 lasagna noodles, uncooked

Snap off tough ends of asparagus. Remove scales from stalks with a knife or vegetable peeler, if desired. Coarsely chop asparagus. Arrange asparagus in a vegetable steamer over boiling water. Cover and steam 4 to 5 minutes or until crisp-tender. Set aside.

Combine tomato and basil in a medium saucepan. Cook over medium heat 20 minutes; remove from heat, and cool slightly. Position knife blade in food processor bowl; add tomato mixture. Process 20 seconds; set aside.

Coat a large nonstick skillet with cooking spray; add olive oil. Place over medium-high heat until hot. Add parsley and garlic; sauté 1 minute. Add asparagus and chicken broth; simmer, uncovered, 5 minutes. Add ricotta cheese, cream cheese product, and lemon juice; stir well. Cook over medium heat, stirring constantly, until cheeses melt. Stir in Romano cheese and nutmeg. Remove from heat; keep warm.

Cook lasagna noodles according to package directions, omitting salt and fat; drain.

Coat an 11- x 7- x 1½-inch baking dish with cooking spray. Place 2 lasagna noodles in bottom of dish; top with half of asparagus mixture. Place 2 lasagna noodles over asparagus mixture; top with half of tomato mixture. Repeat layers with remaining noodles and remaining asparagus mixture. Top with remaining tomato mixture. Cover and bake 10 minutes at 375°. Uncover and bake an additional 15 minutes or until thoroughly heated. Yield: 8 servings.

PER SERVING: 242 CALORIES (22% FROM FAT)
FAT 5.8G (SATURATED FAT 2.6G)
PROTEIN 20.6G   CARBOHYDRATE 30.8G
CHOLESTEROL 22MG   SODIUM 352MG

LINGUINE WITH ASPARAGUS AND GOAT CHEESE

½ pound fresh asparagus
½ cup canned no-salt-added chicken broth,
    undiluted
¼ cup Chablis or other dry white wine
¼ cup chopped shallots
¼ teaspoon pepper
½ (8-ounce) package Neufchâtel cheese, softened
2 ounces goat cheese, crumbled
2 tablespoons fresh lemon juice
8 ounces linguine, uncooked
½ cup thinly sliced sweet red pepper

Snap off tough ends of asparagus. Remove scales from stalks with a knife or vegetable peeler, if desired. Cut asparagus into 1-inch pieces. Set aside.

Combine chicken broth, white wine, shallots, and ¼ teaspoon pepper in a saucepan. Bring to a boil; add asparagus. Reduce heat, and simmer 5 minutes. Add cheeses and lemon juice; cook over low heat, stirring constantly, until cheeses melt. Set aside, and keep warm.

Cook pasta according to package directions, omitting salt and fat; drain. Place pasta in a serving bowl. Add asparagus mixture and sweet red pepper; toss gently. Serve immediately. Yield: 5 (1-cup) servings.

PER SERVING: 305 CALORIES (31% FROM FAT)
FAT 10.4G (SATURATED FAT 6.3G)
PROTEIN 13.3G   CARBOHYDRATE 40.0G
CHOLESTEROL 29MG   SODIUM 149MG

BEANS WITH ORZO PRIMAVERA

Vegetable cooking spray
1 teaspoon cumin seeds, crushed
¾ cup chopped onion
2 teaspoons minced garlic
2 teaspoons olive oil
1 (15-ounce) can black beans, drained
1 (16-ounce) can navy beans, drained
3½ cups canned low-sodium chicken broth, undiluted and divided
1 cup orzo, uncooked
2 teaspoons ground coriander
½ teaspoon ground turmeric
½ teaspoon ground red pepper
1 cup diced zucchini
1 cup cauliflower flowerets
1 cup diced fresh green beans
¾ cup seeded, chopped plum tomato

Coat a large heavy skillet with cooking spray; place over medium-high heat until hot. Add cumin seeds, and cook, stirring constantly, until seeds are fragrant and lightly browned. Add onion, garlic, and olive oil; sauté 3 to 5 minutes or until onion is tender. Stir in beans and 1 cup chicken broth. Bring to a boil; reduce heat, and simmer, uncovered, 15 to 20 minutes or until liquid is absorbed, stirring frequently. Set aside, and keep warm.

Place remaining 2½ cups chicken broth in a medium saucepan; bring to a boil. Add orzo, coriander, turmeric, and red pepper. Cover, reduce heat, and simmer 25 to 30 minutes or until liquid is absorbed and orzo is tender, stirring occasionally. Set aside, and keep warm.

Arrange zucchini, cauliflower, and green beans in a vegetable steamer over boiling water. Cover and steam 2 to 3 minutes or until vegetables are crisp-tender. Combine orzo mixture and zucchini mixture; toss gently. Spoon orzo mixture onto a serving platter; top with bean mixture, and sprinkle with chopped tomato. Yield: 6 servings.

PER SERVING: 286 CALORIES (12% FROM FAT)
FAT 3.8G (SATURATED FAT 0.8G)
PROTEIN 14.5G CARBOHYDRATE 50.4G
CHOLESTEROL 0MG SODIUM 298MG

PASTA E FAGIOLI

1¼ cups dried Great Northern beans
2 quarts water
Olive oil-flavored vegetable cooking spray
1 teaspoon olive oil
½ cup finely chopped red onion
¼ cup finely chopped celery
1 tablespoon minced garlic
2 teaspoons chopped fresh rosemary
2 teaspoons chopped fresh sage
1 cup peeled, seeded, and finely chopped tomato
¼ teaspoon salt
1 teaspoon pepper
8 ounces ditalini (small tubular pasta), uncooked
3 cups coarsely chopped fresh spinach

Sort and wash beans; place in a Dutch oven. Cover with water to a depth of 2 inches above beans; let soak 8 hours. Drain and rinse beans.

Combine beans and 2 quarts water in pan. Bring to a boil; cover, reduce heat, and simmer 1 hour. Transfer 2 cups beans, without liquid, to container of an electric blender or food processor; cover and process until smooth. Return to pan.

Coat a large nonstick skillet with cooking spray; add oil. Place over medium heat until hot; add onion and next 4 ingredients, and sauté 5 minutes. Add onion mixture, tomato, salt, and pepper to bean mixture. Cook over medium-low heat 15 minutes. Add pasta, and cook an additional 20 minutes, stirring frequently. Add spinach, and cook 2 minutes or until spinach wilts. Yield: 8 (1-cup) servings.

PER SERVING: 261 CALORIES (6% FROM FAT)
FAT 1.8G (SATURATED FAT 0.3G)
PROTEIN 13.2G CARBOHYDRATE 49.2G
CHOLESTEROL 0MG SODIUM 98MG

BROCCOLI-CHEESE STUFFED SHELLS

¾ cup 1% low-fat cottage cheese
⅓ cup (1⅓ ounces) shredded part-skim
    mozzarella cheese
¼ cup grated Parmesan cheese
1 (10-ounce) package frozen chopped broccoli,
    thawed and drained
2 teaspoons minced green onions
¼ teaspoon dried whole oregano
⅛ teaspoon white pepper
24 cooked jumbo whole wheat shells (cooked
    without salt or fat)
Vegetable cooking spray
Quick Tomato Sauce

Combine first 7 ingredients in a medium bowl;
stir well.

Stuff each shell with 1 heaping tablespoon of the
broccoli mixture. Arrange shells in a shallow baking
dish coated with cooking spray. Bake at 350° for 15
minutes or until thoroughly heated. Spoon Quick
Tomato Sauce over shells. Yield: 6 servings.

QUICK TOMATO SAUCE
Vegetable cooking spray
¼ cup diced onion
2 (8-ounce) cans no-salt-added tomato sauce
¼ teaspoon salt
⅛ teaspoon garlic powder

Coat a small saucepan with cooking spray; place
over medium heat until hot. Add onion, and sauté
3 minutes or until tender. Stir in remaining ingredients; bring to a boil, stirring constantly. Yield:
1½ cups.

PER SERVING: 186 CALORIES (16% FROM FAT)
FAT 3.4G (SATURATED FAT 1.8G)
PROTEIN 12.0G CARBOHYDRATE 27.2G
CHOLESTEROL 8MG SODIUM 358MG

EGGPLANT LINGUINE

8 ounces linguine, uncooked
Vegetable cooking spray
2 cups peeled, cubed eggplant
½ cup sliced fresh mushrooms
¾ cup Burgundy or other dry red wine
¼ cup sun-dried tomato tidbits
1½ teaspoons sugar
1 (27.5-ounce) jar reduced-fat, reduced-sodium
    tomato-and-herbs pasta sauce
¼ cup chopped fresh parsley
¼ cup grated Parmesan cheese

Cook pasta according to package directions, omitting salt and fat. Drain pasta, and set aside.

Coat a nonstick skillet with cooking spray; place
over medium-high heat until hot. Add eggplant and
mushrooms; sauté 3 minutes. Add wine; cook 2
minutes. Add tomato tidbits, sugar, and pasta
sauce; reduce heat, and simmer 5 minutes.

For each serving, spoon 1 cup sauce over 1 cup
pasta; sprinkle with 1 tablespoon parsley and 1
tablespoon cheese. Yield: 4 servings.

PER SERVING: 357 CALORIES (11% FROM FAT)
FAT 4.5G (SATURATED FAT 1.8G)
PROTEIN 14.3G CARBOHYDRATE 64.5G
CHOLESTEROL 12MG SODIUM 845MG

FYI

Sun-dried tomatoes are a great addition to
pasta entrées, side dishes, and salads. They
are available packed in oil or dry-packed, salt-
ed or not. It is usually recommended that the
dried type be soaked or cooked in water or
another liquid before being served.

Eggplant Linguine

Macaroni with Eggplant, Olives, and Thyme

1 (1-pound) eggplant
¼ teaspoon salt
Vegetable cooking spray
2 teaspoons olive oil
5 plum tomatoes, seeded and cut into thin
   strips
2 tablespoons chopped fresh thyme
12 ounces small elbow macaroni, uncooked
3 ounces smoked mozzarella cheese, diced
3 ounces part-skim mozzarella cheese, diced
¼ cup sliced pimiento-stuffed olives
3 tablespoons grated Parmesan cheese

Peel eggplant; cut into ½-inch-thick slices. Cut slices into ¼-inch-wide strips. Place in a colander; sprinkle with salt. Let stand 1 hour. Pat dry with paper towels.

Coat a large nonstick skillet with cooking spray; add olive oil. Place over medium-high heat until hot. Add eggplant, and sauté until eggplant is tender and lightly browned. Add tomato and thyme; sauté 2 minutes.

Cook macaroni according to package directions, omitting salt and fat; drain. Combine macaroni and eggplant mixture; stir in mozzarella cheeses. Spoon mixture into a 3-quart casserole; sprinkle with olives and Parmesan cheese. Bake at 350° for 20 to 25 minutes or until thoroughly heated. Yield: 8 servings.

Per Serving: 256 Calories (24% from fat)
Fat 6.9g (Saturated Fat 3.1g)
Protein 11.7g Carbohydrate 36.8g
Cholesterol 16mg Sodium 459mg

Eggplant Manicotti and Spinach Sauce

1 medium eggplant (about 1 pound)
2 cloves garlic, thinly sliced
1 medium-size sweet red pepper
3 large plum tomatoes (about ¾ pound)
1 teaspoon dried whole thyme
¼ teaspoon salt
8 cooked manicotti shells (cooked without salt
   or fat)
Vegetable cooking spray
3 cups tightly packed torn fresh spinach (about
   ¼ pound)
½ cup 1% low-fat cottage cheese
1 tablespoon lemon juice
¼ teaspoon pepper
3 tablespoons freshly grated Parmesan cheese

Make several ½-inch slits on outside of eggplant; insert garlic slices. Bake at 350° for 1 hour; let cool. Peel eggplant, and cut into 1-inch cubes.

Cut sweet red pepper in half lengthwise; discard seeds and membranes. Place pepper, skin side up, on a baking sheet; flatten with palm of hand. Broil 3 inches from heat (with electric oven door partially opened) 10 minutes or until charred. Place in ice water; let stand 5 minutes. Remove from water; peel and discard skin.

Position knife blade in food processor bowl; add eggplant, sweet red pepper, tomato, thyme, and salt. Process mixture until chopped. Stuff each shell with ⅓ cup eggplant mixture. Arrange stuffed shells in a baking dish coated with cooking spray. Cover and bake at 350° for 30 minutes.

Wash food processor bowl and blade. Position blade in bowl. Combine spinach and next 3 ingredients in food processor bowl; process until smooth. Spoon spinach mixture over shells, and sprinkle with Parmesan cheese. Cover and let stand 5 minutes. Yield: 4 servings.

Per Serving: 216 Calories (12% from fat)
Fat 2.9g (Saturated Fat 1.2g)
Protein 12.3g Carbohydrate 37.4g
Cholesterol 5mg Sodium 384mg

TORTELLINI WITH ZUCCHINI AND SUN-DRIED TOMATOES

*You may use regular vegetable cooking spray
if you do not have the olive oil-flavored spray
on hand.*

¼ cup sun-dried tomatoes (without salt or oil)
½ cup hot water
Olive oil-flavored vegetable cooking spray
1 tablespoon olive oil
1 cup chopped zucchini
3 cloves garlic, minced
2 green onions, cut into 1-inch pieces
¼ cup chopped sweet red pepper
1 teaspoon dried whole oregano
1 (9-ounce) package fresh cheese tortellini

Combine tomato and water in a small bowl; cover
and let stand 15 minutes. Drain tomato, and slice
thinly; set aside.

Coat a large nonstick skillet with cooking spray;
add olive oil. Place over medium-high heat until
hot. Add zucchini and garlic; sauté 2 minutes. Add
green onions, sweet red pepper, and oregano; sauté
1 minute. Stir in tomato. Remove from heat, and
keep warm.

Cook tortellini according to package directions,
omitting salt and fat; drain well. Place tortellini in a
serving bowl. Add zucchini mixture; toss gently.
Serve immediately. Yield: 4 (1-cup) servings.

PER SERVING: 249 CALORIES (25% FROM FAT)
FAT 6.9G (SATURATED FAT 2.0G)
PROTEIN 12.1G CARBOHYDRATE 47.7G
CHOLESTEROL 29MG SODIUM 434MG

MACARONI AND CHEESE WITH VEGETABLES

1 cup medium shell macaroni, uncooked
½ cup coarsely shredded carrot
½ cup coarsely shredded zucchini
1 tablespoon finely chopped green onions
1 teaspoon cornstarch
¼ teaspoon paprika
⅛ teaspoon salt
⅛ teaspoon dry mustard
⅛ teaspoon pepper
½ cup 2% low-fat milk
½ cup (2 ounces) shredded reduced-fat
    Monterey Jack cheese

Cook macaroni in boiling water 10 minutes, omitting salt and fat. Add carrot, zucchini, and green
onions; cook 1 minute. Drain well; place pasta mixture in a bowl, and set aside.

Combine cornstarch and next 4 ingredients in a
small saucepan. Gradually add milk, stirring with a
wire whisk. Bring to a boil over medium heat, stirring constantly; cook 1 minute. Remove from heat;
stir in cheese. Pour over pasta mixture; toss gently.
Serve warm. Yield: 2 servings.

PER SERVING: 374 CALORIES (19% FROM FAT)
FAT 7.7G (SATURATED FAT 4.0G)
PROTEIN 19.3G CARBOHYDRATE 56.4G
CHOLESTEROL 23MG SODIUM 367MG

Lighten Up

By substituting certain ingredients, you can
make your family's favorite recipes healthier.
For example, something as basic as macaroni
and cheese becomes more nutritious with a few
simple changes. When you replace the cheese
and whole milk in the traditional recipe with
reduced-fat cheese and skim or low-fat milk,
you reduce the calories, fat, and cholesterol.

RAVIOLI WITH CILANTRO-TOMATO SAUCE

1½ cups nonfat ricotta cheese
¼ cup chopped onion
¼ cup canned chopped roasted red pepper in
     water, drained
1 cup (4 ounces) shredded reduced-fat
     Monterey Jack cheese
½ teaspoon ground cumin
60 fresh or frozen wonton skins, thawed
3 quarts water
Cilantro-Tomato Sauce
Fresh cilantro sprigs (optional)

Combine first 5 ingredients in a medium bowl; stir
well. Place 1 tablespoon cheese mixture in center of
each of 30 wonton skins. Brush edges of wonton skins
with water; top with remaining 30 wonton skins.

Press wonton edges together to seal, pushing out
air. Trim wonton edges with a fluted pastry wheel,
if desired.

Bring 3 quarts water to a boil in a Dutch oven.
Add one-third of ravioli, and return water to a boil;
reduce heat, and simmer 5 minutes or until ravioli
are tender. Remove ravioli with a slotted spoon.
Repeat procedure with remaining ravioli.

Spoon Cilantro-Tomato Sauce evenly onto 6
individual serving plates. Place 5 ravioli on each
plate. Garnish with cilantro sprigs, if desired. Serve
immediately. Yield: 6 servings.

CILANTRO-TOMATO SAUCE
Vegetable cooking spray
½ cup minced onion
1 clove garlic, minced
2 (8-ounce) cans no-salt-added tomato sauce
1 (4-ounce) can chopped green chiles, drained
⅓ cup minced fresh cilantro
1 teaspoon sugar
¼ teaspoon salt

Coat a medium saucepan with cooking spray;
place over medium-high heat until hot. Add onion
and garlic; sauté 3 minutes or until tender. Add
tomato sauce and remaining ingredients; stir well.

Reduce heat, and cook, uncovered, 20 minutes,
stirring occasionally. Serve warm. Yield: 2½ cups.

PER SERVING: 380 CALORIES (12% FROM FAT)
FAT 5.1G (SATURATED FAT 2.3G)
PROTEIN 23.4G   CARBOHYDRATE 61.7G
CHOLESTEROL 26MG   SODIUM 802MG

SPINACH-RICOTTA STUFFED SHELLS

*Whole wheat rolls and a fresh fruit salad make
ideal accompaniments to this light main dish.*

Vegetable cooking spray
1 cup chopped onion
6 cups chopped fresh spinach (about ½ pound)
1¼ cups minced cabbage (about ¼ pound)
2 tablespoons Chablis or other dry white wine
⅔ cup part-skim ricotta cheese
2 tablespoons minced fresh parsley
¼ teaspoon pepper, divided
15 cooked jumbo macaroni shells (cooked
     without salt or fat)
1 (10½-ounce) can no-salt-added chicken
     broth
1 (6-ounce) can tomato paste
¼ teaspoon salt
¼ teaspoon ground nutmeg

Coat a large skillet with cooking spray; place over
medium heat until hot. Add chopped onion, and
sauté until tender. Add spinach, cabbage, and wine;
sauté 4 minutes. Stir in ricotta cheese, parsley, and
⅛ teaspoon pepper; sauté 2 minutes. Stuff each
macaroni shell with 2½ tablespoons spinach mixture; arrange in a shallow baking dish coated with
cooking spray, and set aside.

Combine remaining ⅛ teaspoon pepper, broth,
and remaining ingredients in a small bowl. Spoon
over shells; cover and bake at 350° for 30 minutes
or until thoroughly heated. Yield: 5 servings.

PER SERVING: 185 CALORIES (20% FROM FAT)
FAT 4.2G (SATURATED FAT 1.8G)
PROTEIN 10.0G   CARBOHYDRATE 28.6G
CHOLESTEROL 10MG   SODIUM 257MG

Spinach-Ricotta Stuffed Shells

Vegetable Lasagna

VEGETABLE LASAGNA

1 (8-ounce) package light cream cheese
    product, at room temperature
¾ cup nonfat ricotta cheese
½ cup nonfat sour cream alternative
¼ cup frozen egg substitute, thawed
¼ cup grated Parmesan cheese
2 teaspoons dried Italian seasoning
1 (14½-ounce) can no-salt-added whole
    tomatoes, coarsely chopped
1 (6-ounce) can no-salt-added tomato paste
¼ cup chopped fresh parsley
¼ cup red wine vinegar
1 clove garlic, minced
1 teaspoon dried whole oregano
½ teaspoon freshly ground black pepper
Vegetable cooking spray
4 large carrots, scraped and grated
3 cups sliced fresh mushrooms
1 large zucchini, chopped
1 cup chopped onion
4 large cloves garlic, minced
6 cooked lasagna noodles (cooked without salt
    or fat)
1 cup (4 ounces) shredded part-skim
    mozzarella cheese
1 (6-ounce) package part-skim mozzarella
    cheese slices, cut into ½-inch-wide strips
Fresh oregano sprigs (optional)

Beat cream cheese product in a medium bowl at medium speed of an electric mixer until light and fluffy. Add ricotta cheese and next 4 ingredients; beat until smooth. Set aside.

Combine tomato and next 6 ingredients in a medium saucepan; bring to a boil. Reduce heat to low; cover and simmer 10 minutes.

Coat a large skillet with cooking spray, and place over medium-high heat until hot. Add carrot, and sauté 5 to 6 minutes or until tender. Remove carrot from skillet, and set aside. Sauté mushrooms, zucchini, onion, and minced garlic in skillet until tender; add carrot. Remove from heat, and set vegetable mixture aside.

Coat a 13- x 9- x 2-inch baking dish with cooking spray. Layer half each of the lasagna noodles, cheese mixture, vegetable mixture, and tomato mixture in dish. Sprinkle with shredded mozzarella. Repeat all layers except cheese. Cover and bake at 350° for 20 to 25 minutes or until thoroughly heated.

Uncover and arrange strips of mozzarella in a lattice design over lasagna. Bake 10 additional minutes. Let stand 10 minutes. Garnish with fresh oregano, if desired. Yield: 10 servings.

PER SERVING: 265 CALORIES (33% FROM FAT)
FAT 9.8G (SATURATED FAT 5.8G)
PROTEIN 18.4G CARBOHYDRATE 27.3G
CHOLESTEROL 34MG SODIUM 366MG

Keep sodium and fat low by cooking the lasagna noodles according to package directions, omitting salt and fat.

Layer the noodles, cheese mixture, vegetable mixture, and tomato mixture in a dish coated with cooking spray.

Use a fluted pastry wheel or pizza cutter to cut the mozzarella cheese slices into thin strips for the lattice topping.

ON THE SIDE

One generation ago, a well-balanced meal always included potatoes or rice. But times change. Following the lead of many chefs, today's cooks favor pasta as a starchy side dish. And why not? The variety of pasta shapes and sizes adds interest to a menu, and the carbohydrate-rich content, along with little or no fat, makes it healthy, too.

In the first few pages are several simple recipes like Caraway Fettuccine (page 106). Further into this chapter, you'll find recipes, such as Bow Tie Pasta Primavera (page 114) and Spaghetti-Vegetable Toss (page 120), that incorporate a few more ingredients.

Bow Tie Pasta Primavera (Recipe follows on page 114)

ANGEL HAIR PASTA WITH PIMIENTO

1 (4-ounce) jar sliced pimiento, undrained
4 ounces capellini (angel hair pasta), uncooked
2 tablespoons grated Parmesan cheese
1 tablespoon chopped chives
1 teaspoon olive oil
Dash of garlic powder

Drain pimiento, reserving 1 teaspoon juice; set pimiento and reserved juice aside.

Break pasta into thirds; cook according to package directions, omitting salt and fat; drain. Place pasta in a serving bowl. Add pimiento, reserved pimiento juice, cheese, and remaining ingredients; toss well. Serve warm. Yield: 4 servings.

PER SERVING: 133 CALORIES (16% FROM FAT)
FAT 2.4G (SATURATED FAT 0.7G)
PROTEIN 5.0G CARBOHYDRATE 22.8G
CHOLESTEROL 2MG SODIUM 53MG

CARAWAY FETTUCCINE

⅓ cup evaporated skimmed milk
⅓ cup Chablis or other dry white wine
1½ tablespoons reduced-calorie margarine
3 cups cooked fettuccine (cooked without salt or fat)
3 tablespoons minced fresh parsley
2 teaspoons caraway seeds
¼ teaspoon salt
⅛ teaspoon garlic powder

Combine milk, wine, and margarine in a saucepan; place over medium heat. Cook, stirring constantly, until margarine melts. Add fettuccine and remaining ingredients. Cook, tossing gently, until thoroughly heated. Yield: 4 (¾-cup) servings.

PER SERVING: 193 CALORIES (17% FROM FAT)
FAT 3.7G (SATURATED FAT 0.5G)
PROTEIN 7.0G CARBOHYDRATE 33.3G
CHOLESTEROL 1MG SODIUM 217MG

ORANGE-BASIL LINGUINE

1 tablespoon reduced-calorie margarine, melted
½ cup canned chicken broth, undiluted
½ cup unsweetened orange juice
2 teaspoons cornstarch
1 tablespoon chopped fresh basil
⅛ teaspoon grated orange rind
3 cups hot cooked whole wheat linguine (cooked without salt or fat)
1 tablespoon grated Parmesan cheese
Fresh orange slices (optional)
Fresh basil sprigs (optional)

Combine first 4 ingredients in a small saucepan; stir well. Bring to a boil, and cook 1 minute. Remove from heat. Add chopped basil and orange rind; stir well. Pour over linguine; toss gently to coat. Sprinkle with cheese. Garnish with orange slices and basil sprigs, if desired. Yield: 6 (½-cup) servings.

PER SERVING: 131 CALORIES (21% FROM FAT)
FAT 3.1G (SATURATED FAT 0.6G)
PROTEIN 4.7G CARBOHYDRATE 23.0G
CHOLESTEROL 1MG SODIUM 104MG

FYI

Fresh basil is usually available at large supermarkets and specialty produce stores. This herb bruises easily, so handle it carefully. Cut it with a very sharp, thin-bladed stainless-steel knife. If you use a food processor, a few 3- to 5-second pulses are sufficient for chopping.

Orange-Basil Linguine

DILLED RIGATONI

½ (8-ounce) package Neufchâtel cheese, softened
¼ cup hot water
2 teaspoons chopped green onions
1 teaspoon lemon juice
½ teaspoon dried whole dillweed
¼ teaspoon salt
8 ounces rigatoni (tubular pasta), uncooked

Beat Neufchâtel cheese in a medium bowl at medium speed of an electric mixer until creamy. Gradually add hot water, beating until smooth. Stir in green onions, lemon juice, dillweed, and salt; set aside.

Cook rigatoni according to package directions, omitting salt and fat; drain. Add rigatoni to Neufchâtel mixture, tossing gently. Serve immediately. Yield: 8 servings.

PER SERVING: 143 CALORIES (24% FROM FAT)
FAT 3.8G (SATURATED FAT 2.2G)
PROTEIN 5.1G   CARBOHYDRATE 21.7G
CHOLESTEROL 11MG   SODIUM 132MG

SESAME-PEANUT SAUCED NOODLES

2 small cloves garlic
¼ cup (½-inch) sliced green onions (about 2 medium)
2 tablespoons creamy peanut butter
1½ teaspoons rice vinegar
1½ teaspoons low-sodium soy sauce
1 teaspoon sugar
½ teaspoon dark sesame oil
¼ teaspoon crushed red pepper
Dash of ground ginger
4 cups hot cooked spaghetti (cooked without salt or fat)

Position knife blade in food processor bowl. With processor running, drop garlic through food chute, and process 3 seconds or until garlic is minced. Add green onions and next 7 ingredients, and process 20 seconds or until mixture is smooth, scraping sides of processor bowl once. Toss with spaghetti; serve warm. Yield: 8 (½-cup) servings.

PER SERVING: 130 CALORIES (19% FROM FAT)
FAT 2.8G (SATURATED FAT 0.5G)
PROTEIN 4.6G   CARBOHYDRATE 21.5G
CHOLESTEROL 0MG   SODIUM 46MG

LINGUINE IN SOUR CREAM-WINE SAUCE

6 ounces linguine, uncooked
¼ cup nonfat sour cream alternative
3 tablespoons Chablis or other dry white wine
1½ tablespoons grated Parmesan cheese
⅛ teaspoon salt
⅛ teaspoon pepper
Vegetable cooking spray
1⅓ cups sliced fresh mushrooms
½ cup chopped green onions
1 tablespoon chopped fresh parsley

Cook linguine according to package directions, omitting salt and fat. Drain well. Combine sour cream and next 4 ingredients in a medium bowl; stir well. Add linguine; toss well, and set aside.

Coat a large nonstick skillet with cooking spray; place over medium heat until hot. Add mushrooms and green onions; sauté until tender.

Add linguine mixture; cook, tossing gently, until mixture is thoroughly heated. Transfer linguine mixture to a serving bowl; sprinkle with parsley, and serve immediately. Yield: 4 (¾-cup) servings.

PER SERVING: 186 CALORIES (7% FROM FAT)
FAT 1.5G (SATURATED FAT 0.5G)
PROTEIN 7.8G   CARBOHYDRATE 34.6G
CHOLESTEROL 1MG   SODIUM 125MG

PASTA WITH RED PEPPER SAUCE

Olive oil-flavored vegetable cooking spray
2 teaspoons olive oil
2 cups chopped onion
2 cloves garlic, minced
4¾ cups chopped sweet red pepper (about 4 large)
½ cup canned no-salt-added chicken broth, undiluted
1 tablespoon white wine vinegar
½ teaspoon salt
¼ teaspoon ground white pepper
Dash of crushed red pepper
10 ounces linguine, uncooked
Fresh basil sprigs (optional)

Coat a large Dutch oven with cooking spray; add oil. Place over medium-high heat until hot. Add chopped onion and garlic; sauté until tender. Add sweet red pepper and chicken broth; bring to a boil. Cover, reduce heat, and simmer 15 minutes or until pepper is tender. Remove from heat.

Transfer pepper mixture, in batches, to container of an electric blender or food processor; cover and process until smooth. Return pureed mixture to Dutch oven. Add white wine vinegar, salt, white pepper, and crushed red pepper. Cook over medium-low heat until thoroughly heated.

Cook linguine according to package directions, omitting salt and fat; drain. Place linguine in a large serving bowl. Add red pepper sauce, tossing well. Garnish with fresh basil sprigs, if desired. Yield: 8 (¾-cup) servings.

PER SERVING: 157 CALORIES (15% FROM FAT)
FAT 2.6G (SATURATED FAT 0.2G)
PROTEIN 5.1G CARBOHYDRATE 28.5G
CHOLESTEROL 15MG SODIUM 245MG

WHOLE WHEAT SPAGHETTI WITH TOMATO SAUCE

Vegetable cooking spray
1 cup minced onion
2 cloves garlic, minced
2 tablespoons Burgundy or other dry red wine
1 teaspoon beef-flavored bouillon granules
4½ cups peeled, chopped tomatoes
1 tablespoon minced fresh parsley
2 teaspoons dried Italian seasoning
⅛ to ¼ teaspoon crushed red pepper
2 tablespoons tomato paste
1 (8-ounce) can no-salt-added tomato sauce
1 bay leaf
4 cups hot cooked whole wheat spaghetti (cooked without salt or fat)
1 tablespoon plus 2 teaspoons grated Parmesan cheese
Fresh parsley sprigs (optional)

Coat a Dutch oven with cooking spray; place over medium heat until hot. Add onion and garlic; sauté 3 minutes or until tender. Add wine and next 8 ingredients; stir well, and bring to a boil. Reduce heat, and simmer, uncovered, 1 hour or until sauce is reduced to 4 cups; stir occasionally.

Remove from heat; discard bay leaf. Serve over spaghetti, and sprinkle with cheese. Garnish with parsley, if desired. Yield: 8 (1-cup) servings.

PER SERVING: 154 CALORIES (13% FROM FAT)
FAT 2.3G (SATURATED FAT 0.5G)
PROTEIN 6.1G CARBOHYDRATE 30.3G
CHOLESTEROL 1MG SODIUM 161MG

ALMOND ORZO

2 quarts water
⅔ cup orzo (rice-shaped pasta), uncooked
3 tablespoons grated Parmesan cheese
2 tablespoons blanched slivered almonds,
    toasted
2 tablespoons skim milk
¼ teaspoon salt
⅛ teaspoon paprika

Bring water to a boil in a saucepan. Add orzo; return water to a boil. Cook, uncovered, 10 to 12 minutes or just until orzo is tender; drain well.

Combine cooked orzo, Parmesan cheese, and remaining ingredients in a medium bowl; toss well. Yield: 4 (½-cup) servings.

PER SERVING: 156 CALORIES (18% FROM FAT)
FAT 3.2G (SATURATED FAT 0.9G)
PROTEIN 6.5G CARBOHYDRATE 25.0G
CHOLESTEROL 3MG SODIUM 223MG

CHEESY VEGETABLE ORZO

When fresh basil is not available, substitute ¾ to 1 teaspoon dried whole basil.

Vegetable cooking spray
¼ cup chopped onion
1 clove garlic, minced
½ cup canned low-sodium chicken broth,
    undiluted
¼ cup diced carrot
1 tablespoon chopped fresh basil
⅛ teaspoon salt
⅛ teaspoon pepper
¼ cup orzo (rice-shaped pasta), uncooked
¼ cup shredded zucchini
2 tablespoons shredded reduced-fat sharp
    Cheddar cheese

Coat a small saucepan with cooking spray; place over medium heat until hot. Add onion and garlic; sauté 2 minutes. Add broth and next 4 ingredients; bring to a boil. Add orzo. Cover; reduce heat.

Simmer about 16 minutes. Remove from heat; stir in zucchini and cheese. Cover and let stand 2 minutes. Yield: 2 (½-cup) servings.

PER SERVING: 157 CALORIES (15% FROM FAT)
FAT 2.6G (SATURATED FAT 0.9G)
PROTEIN 7.0G CARBOHYDRATE 26.4G
CHOLESTEROL 5MG SODIUM 226MG

MEDITERRANEAN ORZO

If you don't have all three colors of peppers, use ¾ cup of whatever sweet pepper is on hand.

1 cup orzo (rice-shaped pasta), uncooked
1 cup water
½ ounce sun-dried tomatoes (packed without oil)
¼ cup (1 ounce) crumbled feta cheese
¼ cup chopped purple onion
¼ cup chopped sweet yellow pepper
¼ cup chopped green pepper
¼ cup chopped sweet red pepper
2 tablespoons chopped fresh parsley
2 tablespoons sliced ripe olives
¼ teaspoon pepper
2 tablespoons red wine vinegar
1½ teaspoons olive oil

Cook orzo according to package directions, omitting salt and fat; drain and set aside.

Bring 1 cup water to a boil in a small saucepan. Add tomato; cook 2 minutes or until tender. Drain and chop.

Combine orzo, tomato, feta cheese, and remaining ingredients in a large bowl; toss well. Yield: 4 (1-cup) servings.

PER SERVING: 244 CALORIES (17% FROM FAT)
FAT 4.7G (SATURATED FAT 1.5G)
PROTEIN 8.1G CARBOHYDRATE 42.3G
CHOLESTEROL 6MG SODIUM 123MG

Mediterranean Orzo

LINGUINE WITH ASPARAGUS AND SHIITAKE MUSHROOMS

1 pound fresh asparagus
Olive oil-flavored vegetable cooking spray
1 teaspoon olive oil
3½ ounces fresh shiitake mushrooms, sliced
2 teaspoons minced garlic
½ cup chopped fresh parsley
¼ cup Chablis or other dry white wine
1½ tablespoons lemon juice
¼ teaspoon salt
¼ teaspoon crushed red pepper
6 ounces linguine, uncooked
2 tablespoons grated Parmesan cheese

Snap off tough ends of asparagus. Remove scales from stalks with a knife or vegetable peeler, if desired. Cut asparagus diagonally into ¾-inch pieces.

Coat a nonstick skillet with cooking spray. Add olive oil; place over medium-high heat until hot. Add asparagus, and sauté 1 minute. Add mushrooms and garlic; reduce heat to medium, and cook 3 minutes. Add parsley and next 4 ingredients; cook 2 minutes. Set aside, and keep warm.

Cook linguine according to package directions, omitting salt and fat; drain well. Place linguine in a serving bowl. Add asparagus mixture and Parmesan cheese; toss gently. Serve immediately. Yield: 5 (1-cup) servings.

PER SERVING: 171 CALORIES (13% FROM FAT)
FAT 2.4G (SATURATED FAT 0.7G)
PROTEIN 7.4G   CARBOHYDRATE 30.8G
CHOLESTEROL 2MG   SODIUM 162MG

ROTELLE WITH BROCCOLI

3 cups fresh broccoli flowerets
Vegetable cooking spray
1 tablespoon olive oil
1 tablespoon finely chopped onion
1½ teaspoons drained chopped anchovy fillets
1 teaspoon minced garlic
8 ounces rotelle (corkscrew pasta), uncooked
½ cup grated Romano cheese
¼ cup sliced ripe olives
2 tablespoons chopped fresh basil

Arrange broccoli in a vegetable steamer over boiling water. Cover and steam 5 minutes or until crisp-tender. Set aside.

Coat a large nonstick skillet with cooking spray; add olive oil. Place over medium-high heat until hot. Add onion, anchovies, and garlic; sauté 2 minutes. Add broccoli, and cook until thoroughly heated.

Cook pasta according to package directions, omitting salt and fat; drain well.

Place pasta in a serving bowl. Add broccoli mixture, Romano cheese, olives, and basil; toss gently. Serve immediately. Yield: 8 (1-cup) servings.

PER SERVING: 168 CALORIES (26% FROM FAT)
FAT 4.9G (SATURATED FAT 1.6G)
PROTEIN 7.4G   CARBOHYDRATE 23.8G
CHOLESTEROL 7MG   SODIUM 199MG

FYI

Hot pasta cools quickly when placed on room-temperature serving dishes. To prevent this, run hot water over the serving dishes; then dry them off. The pasta should remain hot once it's transferred to the dishes.

Greek-Style Capellini

GREEK-STYLE CAPELLINI

6 ounces capellini (angel hair pasta), uncooked
1 pound fresh broccoli
Vegetable cooking spray
1 teaspoon olive oil
1 clove garlic, minced
½ cup canned low-sodium chicken broth,
      undiluted
1 teaspoon Greek-style seasoning
2 cups peeled, seeded, and chopped tomato
2 tablespoons sliced ripe olives
¼ teaspoon freshly ground pepper
½ cup (2 ounces) crumbled feta cheese

Prepare capellini according to package directions, omitting salt and fat. Drain well, and set aside.

Trim off large leaves of broccoli; remove tough ends of lower stalks. Wash broccoli thoroughly, and cut into small flowerets; cut stems diagonally into ½-inch pieces.

Coat a large nonstick skillet with cooking spray; add oil. Place over medium-high heat until hot. Add garlic; sauté 1 minute. Add broccoli; sauté until crisp-tender.

Stir broth and Greek-style seasoning into broccoli mixture. Bring to a boil; stir in tomato and capellini. Reduce heat, and simmer until thoroughly heated. Add olives and pepper; toss gently. Transfer to a serving bowl, and sprinkle with cheese. Serve immediately. Yield: 7 (1-cup) servings.

PER SERVING: 149 CALORIES (22% FROM FAT)
FAT 3.6G (SATURATED FAT 1.5G)
PROTEIN 6.3G   CARBOHYDRATE 23.9G
CHOLESTEROL 7MG   SODIUM 316MG

BOW TIE PASTA PRIMAVERA

(pictured on page 104)

½ pound fresh asparagus spears
1½ cups fresh broccoli flowerets
1 large carrot, scraped and diagonally sliced
1 cup sliced yellow squash
Olive oil-flavored vegetable cooking spray
1 teaspoon olive oil
1 cup sliced fresh mushrooms
½ cup chopped onion
½ cup chopped sweet red pepper
1 clove garlic, minced
8 ounces farfalle (bow tie pasta), uncooked
1 tablespoon margarine
1 tablespoon all-purpose flour
¾ cup skim milk
¼ cup canned no-salt-added chicken broth,
   undiluted
¼ cup plus 1 tablespoon freshly grated
   Parmesan cheese, divided
1 tablespoon chopped fresh parsley
1 tablespoon chopped fresh basil
¼ teaspoon salt
¼ teaspoon freshly ground pepper

Snap off tough ends of asparagus. Remove scales from stalks with a knife or vegetable peeler, if desired. Cut spears diagonally into 1-inch pieces.

Arrange asparagus, broccoli, and carrot in a vegetable steamer over boiling water. Cover and steam 5 minutes. Add squash; cover and steam an additional 5 minutes or until vegetables are crisp-tender. Set aside.

Coat a large nonstick skillet with cooking spray; add oil. Place over medium heat until hot. Add mushrooms, onion, sweet red pepper, and garlic; sauté 3 to 5 minutes or until vegetables are tender. Set aside.

Cook pasta according to package directions, omitting salt and fat. Drain well, and set aside.

Melt margarine in a small, heavy saucepan over low heat; add flour, stirring until smooth. Cook 1 minute, stirring constantly. Gradually add milk and chicken broth to mixture, stirring constantly. Cook over medium heat, stirring constantly, until thickened and bubbly.

Combine asparagus mixture, mushroom mixture, and pasta in a large bowl. Add warm sauce, ¼ cup Parmesan cheese, and remaining ingredients; toss well. Transfer to a large serving bowl, and sprinkle with remaining 1 tablespoon Parmesan cheese. Serve warm. Yield: 8 (1-cup) servings.

PER SERVING: 178 CALORIES (20% FROM FAT)
FAT 4.0G (SATURATED FAT 1.2G)
PROTEIN 7.8G CARBOHYDRATE 28.1G
CHOLESTEROL 3MG SODIUM 191MG

EGGPLANT AND DITALINI PASTA

2½ cups peeled, cubed eggplant
¼ teaspoon salt
Olive oil-flavored vegetable cooking spray
1 teaspoon olive oil
⅓ cup chopped onion
2 teaspoons minced garlic
1 (14½-ounce) can no-salt-added whole
   tomatoes, undrained and chopped
¼ cup water
6 ounces ditalini (small tubular pasta), uncooked
¼ cup grated Romano cheese
1 tablespoon chopped fresh parsley

Place eggplant in a colander; sprinkle with salt. Let stand 1 hour. Rinse; pat dry with paper towels.

Coat a large nonstick skillet with cooking spray; add olive oil. Place over medium heat until hot. Add eggplant; cook 6 minutes, stirring frequently. Add onion; cook 3 minutes. Add garlic, and cook, stirring constantly, 1 minute. Stir in tomato and water. Reduce heat; cook, uncovered, 20 minutes.

Cook pasta according to package directions, omitting salt and fat; drain. Place pasta in a serving bowl. Add eggplant mixture, and toss gently. Sprinkle with cheese and parsley. Serve immediately. Yield: 5 (1-cup) servings.

PER SERVING: 193 CALORIES (15% FROM FAT)
FAT 3.2G (SATURATED FAT 1.2G)
PROTEIN 7.6G CARBOHYDRATE 34.0G
CHOLESTEROL 6MG SODIUM 202MG

MEDITERRANEAN LINGUINE

Vegetable cooking spray
1 cup sliced fresh mushrooms
1 medium-size green pepper, seeded and cut
　　into thin strips
1 medium-size sweet red pepper, seeded and
　　cut into thin strips
1 clove garlic, minced
1 (14-ounce) can artichoke hearts, drained and
　　quartered
½ cup commercial reduced-calorie Italian
　　dressing
3 tablespoons sliced, pitted ripe olives
1 tablespoon chopped fresh parsley
6 ounces linguine, uncooked
½ cup (2 ounces) shredded part-skim
　　mozzarella cheese

Coat a large nonstick skillet with cooking spray; place over medium-high heat until hot. Add mushrooms and next 3 ingredients; sauté until vegetables are crisp-tender. Add artichokes, Italian dressing, olives, and parsley; cook 3 minutes or until thoroughly heated, stirring occasionally.

Cook linguine according to package directions, omitting salt and fat; drain well. Combine linguine and vegetable mixture; toss well. Transfer mixture to a serving dish; sprinkle with cheese, and serve immediately. Yield: 8 (⅔-cup) servings.

PER SERVING: 128 CALORIES (18% FROM FAT)
FAT 2.6G (SATURATED FAT 1.0G)
PROTEIN 6.1G CARBOHYDRATE 22.4G
CHOLESTEROL 4MG SODIUM 317MG

Mediterranean Linguine

Linguine Florentine

LINGUINE FLORENTINE

2 pounds fresh spinach
2 cups hot cooked linguine (cooked without
   salt or fat)
2 teaspoons olive oil
½ cup grated Parmesan cheese
¼ teaspoon pepper
1 tablespoon chopped walnuts

Remove stems from spinach; wash leaves thoroughly. Cook spinach, covered, in a large Dutch oven over medium heat about 4 minutes or until tender. (Do not add water.) Drain spinach well; finely chop leaves, and set aside.

Combine linguine and olive oil in a large bowl, and toss gently. Add spinach, cheese, and pepper; toss gently. Sprinkle with walnuts. Yield: 6 (¾-cup) servings.

PER SERVING: 157 CALORIES (30% FROM FAT)
FAT 5.2G (SATURATED FAT 2.1G)
PROTEIN 10.8G CARBOHYDRATE 19.1G
CHOLESTEROL 7MG SODIUM 296MG

Quick Tip

Pasta may be cooked in advance, tossed lightly with olive oil, if desired, and stored in a covered container in the refrigerator for up to three days. To reheat, place pasta in a colander, and pour boiling water over it. Or bring water to a boil in a saucepan, drop in the cooked pasta, and remove from heat. After the pasta is warm, drain and serve it as usual.

WINE-BRAISED PEPPERS WITH NOODLES

1 large sweet red pepper
1 large sweet yellow pepper
Vegetable cooking spray
1½ teaspoons olive oil
1 medium-size yellow onion, cut into ¾-inch-
   thick slices
¼ cup Chablis or other dry white wine
4 ounces wide noodles, uncooked
1 tablespoon minced fresh parsley
1 tablespoon chopped fresh basil
1 teaspoon balsamic vinegar
¼ teaspoon salt
¼ teaspoon freshly ground pepper

Wash and dry peppers. Place peppers on a baking sheet. Broil 4 inches from heat (with electric oven door partially opened) 2 to 3 minutes on each side or until skins are blackened and charred. Immediately transfer peppers to a large brown paper bag. Roll top tightly to trap steam; let peppers steam 20 minutes. Unroll top, and allow steam to escape; carefully remove peppers. Remove and discard skins and seeds. Cut peppers into ¾-inch strips; set aside.

Coat a large nonstick skillet with cooking spray; add oil. Place over medium-high heat until hot. Add onion, and sauté until tender. Add pepper strips and wine. Bring to a boil; reduce heat, and simmer 1 minute. Cover and simmer an additional 5 minutes.

Cook noodles according to package directions, omitting salt and fat; drain. Combine noodles, pepper mixture, parsley, and remaining ingredients, tossing gently. Yield: 6 (⅔-cup) servings.

PER SERVING: 113 CALORIES (18% FROM FAT)
FAT 2.3G (SATURATED FAT 0.4G)
PROTEIN 3.4G CARBOHYDRATE 18.7G
CHOLESTEROL 18MG SODIUM 105MG

CORKSCREW PASTA TOSS

3 tablespoons sun-dried tomatoes (without salt
    or oil)
1¾ cups diced tomato
½ cup sliced green onions
2 teaspoons olive oil
1 tablespoon white wine vinegar
¼ teaspoon garlic powder
¼ teaspoon ground white pepper
6 ounces tri-colored rotini (corkscrew pasta),
    uncooked
2 tablespoons minced fresh basil
1 cup (4 ounces) shredded part-skim
    mozzarella cheese

Place sun-dried tomatoes in a small bowl; cover
with hot water. Let stand 15 minutes. Drain well;
mince tomato.

Combine minced tomato, diced tomato, and next
5 ingredients in a large bowl. Cover and let stand at
room temperature 2 hours.

Cook pasta according to package directions, omitting salt and fat; drain well.

Add hot pasta and basil to tomato mixture; toss well.
Top with shredded cheese. Yield: 8 (⅔-cup) servings.

PER SERVING: 143 CALORIES (25% FROM FAT)
FAT 4.0G (SATURATED FAT 1.7G)
PROTEIN 7.0G CARBOHYDRATE 20.1G
CHOLESTEROL 8MG SODIUM 128MG

TOMATO-HERB RIGATONI

2 cups peeled, seeded, chopped tomato
¼ cup chopped fresh parsley
2 tablespoons shredded fresh basil
1½ teaspoons minced garlic
1½ tablespoons fresh lemon juice
1½ teaspoons olive oil
½ teaspoon chopped fresh mint
½ teaspoon pepper
¼ teaspoon crushed red pepper
⅛ teaspoon salt
8 ounces rigatoni (tubular pasta), uncooked
Fresh basil sprigs (optional)

Combine first 10 ingredients in a large bowl. Let
stand at room temperature 1 hour.

Cook pasta according to package directions, omitting salt and fat; drain. Add pasta to tomato mixture,
and toss well. Garnish with fresh basil sprigs, if
desired. Serve immediately. Yield: 8 (⅔-cup) servings.

PER SERVING: 124 CALORIES (11% FROM FAT)
FAT 1.5G (SATURATED FAT 0.2G)
PROTEIN 4.1G CARBOHYDRATE 23.7G
CHOLESTEROL 0MG SODIUM 44MG

VEGETABLE RADIATORE

Vegetable cooking spray
½ cup chopped onion
2 cloves garlic, minced
2 cups canned low-sodium chicken broth,
    undiluted
1 medium carrot, scraped and cut into julienne
    strips
2 tablespoons chopped fresh basil
⅛ teaspoon salt
⅛ teaspoon pepper
2¾ ounces (about 1 cup) tri-colored radiatore
    (short, fat rippled pasta), uncooked
1 medium zucchini, cut into julienne strips
¼ cup (1 ounce) shredded reduced-fat sharp
    Cheddar cheese
Fresh basil sprigs (optional)

Coat a large saucepan with cooking spray; place
over medium heat until hot. Add onion and garlic;
sauté until tender. Add broth and next 4 ingredients; bring to a boil. Stir in pasta. Cover, reduce
heat, and simmer 20 to 25 minutes or until pasta is
tender, stirring occasionally; drain.

Stir zucchini and cheese into hot pasta. Cover
and let stand 2 minutes or until cheese melts.
Transfer to a serving dish. Garnish with fresh basil
sprigs, if desired. Yield: 6 (½-cup) servings.

Note: 1 cup uncooked rotini (corkscrew pasta)
may be substituted for radiatore, if desired.

PER SERVING: 84 CALORIES (17% FROM FAT)
FAT 1.6G (SATURATED FAT 0.7G)
PROTEIN 4.0G CARBOHYDRATE 13.7G
CHOLESTEROL 3MG SODIUM 101MG

Vegetable Radiatore

ITALIAN-STYLE TOMATOES AND PASTA

2 teaspoons olive oil
3 cloves garlic, minced
2 pounds ripe plum tomatoes, peeled, seeded, and cut into quarters
3 tablespoons minced fresh parsley
3 tablespoons minced fresh basil
½ teaspoon salt
¼ teaspoon freshly ground pepper
2 tablespoons canned low-sodium chicken broth, undiluted
4 ounces thin spaghetti or vermicelli, uncooked

Heat oil in a nonstick skillet over medium heat until hot; add garlic, and sauté 2 minutes. Add tomato and next 5 ingredients; cook until thoroughly heated, stirring occasionally. Set aside; keep warm.

Cook pasta according to package directions, omitting salt and fat; drain well. Combine pasta and tomato mixture, tossing gently. Serve warm or at room temperature. Yield: 4 (1-cup) servings.

PER SERVING: 175 CALORIES (17% FROM FAT)
FAT 3.4G (SATURATED FAT 0.5G)
PROTEIN 5.7G   CARBOHYDRATE 32.0G
CHOLESTEROL 0MG   SODIUM 317MG

GAZPACHO PASTA

6 ounces spaghetti, uncooked
Vegetable cooking spray
1 cup broccoli flowerets
1 cup thinly sliced carrot
1 cup sliced zucchini
¼ cup sliced onion
1 sweet yellow pepper, cut into julienne strips
½ cup sliced cucumber
½ cup sliced fresh mushrooms
1 small tomato, cut into wedges
2 tablespoons dry vermouth
¼ cup plus 2 tablespoons grated Parmesan cheese
1 tablespoon minced fresh parsley
¼ teaspoon sweet red pepper flakes

Cook pasta according to package directions, omitting salt and fat. Drain and set aside.

Coat a large nonstick skillet with cooking spray; place over medium heat until hot. Add broccoli and next 3 ingredients; sauté 4 minutes. Add pepper strips, cucumber, and mushrooms; sauté 4 minutes or until vegetables are crisp-tender. Add cooked pasta, tomato, and vermouth; toss gently. Cook until heated. Sprinkle with cheese, parsley, and pepper; toss gently. Yield: 6 (1-cup) servings.

PER SERVING: 160 CALORIES (14% FROM FAT)
FAT 2.4G (SATURATED FAT 1.1G)
PROTEIN 7.2G   CARBOHYDRATE 28.1G
CHOLESTEROL 4MG   SODIUM 111MG

SPAGHETTI-VEGETABLE TOSS

Vegetable cooking spray
2 teaspoons olive oil
1 cup fresh broccoli flowerets
1 cup fresh cauliflower flowerets
1 cup julienne-cut carrots
1 cup julienne-cut zucchini
1 tablespoon plus 1 teaspoon minced garlic
1 cup snow pea pods, trimmed
¼ cup canned no-salt-added chicken broth
1 cup cherry tomatoes, halved
8 ounces spaghetti, uncooked
2 tablespoons pine nuts, toasted
2 tablespoons chopped fresh parsley

Coat a large nonstick skillet with cooking spray; add oil. Place over medium-high heat until hot. Add broccoli and next 4 ingredients; sauté 4 minutes. Stir in snow peas and chicken broth. Cover, reduce heat, and cook 6 minutes. Stir in tomato halves, and cook an additional 3 minutes.

Cook pasta according to package directions, omitting salt and fat; drain. Add pasta to vegetable mixture; toss well. Sprinkle with pine nuts and parsley. Serve immediately. Yield: 8 (1-cup) servings.

PER SERVING: 161 CALORIES (21% FROM FAT)
FAT 3.7G (SATURATED FAT 0.5G)
PROTEIN 6.0G   CARBOHYDRATE 27.1G
CHOLESTEROL 0MG   SODIUM 18MG

Spaghetti-Vegetable Toss

PASTA COLD

*W*hen it comes to pasta served cold, the possibilities seem almost endless. Pasta can star as a cold appetizer in Tortellini-Vegetable Kabobs (page 125) or in a variety of side-dish salads (starting on page 126).

For a colorful salad, try combining pasta with vegetables or fruit. The latter may surprise you, but tossed with a slightly sweet yogurt dressing the pasta-fruit combos (page 134) are a refreshing addition to warm weather meals.

To round out this chapter, we've included recipes that combine cold pasta with chicken or fish—ideal as a main dish salad for lunch or a casual supper. You may try substituting one of these for Pasta with Ham and Artichokes (page 23) in the menu for a Neighborhood Supper.

Tuna and Pasta Salad (Recipe follows on page 140)

Tortellini-Vegetable Kabobs

TORTELLINI-VEGETABLE KABOBS

48 small fresh spinach tortellini with cheese, uncooked
24 small fresh cheese tortellini, uncooked
1 teaspoon cornstarch
1 teaspoon dried whole basil
1 teaspoon dried whole oregano
½ teaspoon sugar
½ teaspoon dry mustard
¼ teaspoon onion powder
¼ teaspoon garlic powder
¼ teaspoon salt
⅔ cup water
½ cup cider vinegar
1 (14-ounce) can artichoke hearts, drained
12 small cherry tomatoes, halved
Fresh oregano sprigs (optional)

Cook tortellini according to package directions, omitting salt and fat. Drain and set aside.

Combine cornstarch and next 7 ingredients in a saucepan; gradually stir in water and vinegar. Bring to a boil; cook 30 seconds, stirring with a wire whisk. Remove from heat; let cool.

Cut 6 artichoke hearts into quarters; reserve remaining artichoke hearts for another use. Alternate tortellini, artichoke quarters, and tomato halves on 24 (6-inch) wooden skewers; place in a 13- x 9- x 2-inch baking dish. Pour vinegar mixture over kabobs, turning to coat. Cover and marinate in refrigerator at least 4 hours, turning occasionally.

Drain well, discarding marinade. Transfer kabobs to a serving platter. Garnish with fresh oregano, if desired. Yield: 24 appetizers.

PER APPETIZER: 35 CALORIES (13% FROM FAT)
FAT 0.5G (SATURATED FAT 0.2G)
PROTEIN 1.8G CARBOHYDRATE 6.6G
CHOLESTEROL 4MG SODIUM 56MG

PARTY ANTIPASTO

1 (9-ounce) package fresh cheese tortellini, uncooked
1 (15-ounce) can garbanzo beans, drained
1 (14-ounce) can artichoke hearts, drained and quartered
1 (11½-ounce) jar pepperoncini peppers, drained
1 pint small cherry tomatoes
1 (8-ounce) package small fresh mushrooms
1 cup julienne-cut carrot
1 cup julienne-cut celery
1 cup julienne-cut green pepper
1 cup julienne-cut yellow squash
½ cup whole ripe olives
Antipasto Vinaigrette

Cook tortellini according to package directions, omitting salt and fat; drain well.

Combine cooked tortellini, garbanzo beans, and next 9 ingredients in a large bowl. Pour Antipasto Vinaigrette over vegetable mixture; toss gently to coat. Cover and chill mixture at least 4 hours.

Transfer mixture to a large serving bowl, using a slotted spoon. Yield: 24 (½-cup) appetizer servings.

ANTIPASTO VINAIGRETTE
⅔ cup canned low-sodium chicken broth, undiluted
¼ cup white wine vinegar
1 (2-ounce) jar diced pimiento, drained
1 tablespoon dried Italian seasoning
2 tablespoons lemon juice
2 teaspoons sugar
2 teaspoons Dijon mustard
2 teaspoons olive oil
½ teaspoon garlic powder
½ teaspoon salt

Combine all ingredients in a jar; cover tightly, and shake vigorously to blend. Shake vinaigrette well before serving. Yield: 1⅓ cups.

PER SERVING: 75 CALORIES (22% FROM FAT)
FAT 1.8G (SATURATED FAT 0.4G)
PROTEIN 3.4G CARBOHYDRATE 12.0G
CHOLESTEROL 5MG SODIUM 213MG

MARINATED PASTA SALAD

If you don't have bow tie pasta in the pantry, ziti or rigatoni is a good substitute.

3 ounces farfalle (bow tie pasta), uncooked
1 cup chopped tomato
1 small onion, thinly sliced
3 tablespoons pitted small ripe olives, halved
1 tablespoon chopped fresh parsley
1 tablespoon white wine vinegar
2 teaspoons olive oil
½ teaspoon dried whole basil
½ teaspoon dried whole oregano
½ teaspoon pepper
¼ teaspoon salt
Fresh basil leaves (optional)

Cook pasta according to package directions, omitting salt and fat; drain. Rinse with cold water, and drain again.

Combine pasta, tomato, and next 9 ingredients in a medium bowl; toss gently. Cover and chill at least 2 hours. Garnish with fresh basil, if desired. Yield: 4 (1-cup) servings.

PER SERVING: 132 CALORIES (27% FROM FAT)
FAT 4.0G (SATURATED FAT 0.6G)
PROTEIN 3.9G CARBOHYDRATE 20.9G
CHOLESTEROL 20MG SODIUM 204MG

FYI

You can extend the life of fresh parsley or cilantro by placing the herb in a glass jar with a small amount of water. Cover the jar tightly and refrigerate, changing the water at least every five days.

TRI-PASTA SALAD WITH HERBED VINAIGRETTE

3 ounces ziti (tubular pasta), uncooked
3 ounces farfalle (bow tie pasta), uncooked
3 ounces spinach rotini (corkscrew pasta), uncooked
½ cup chopped green pepper
½ cup chopped sweet red pepper
½ cup chopped sweet yellow pepper
½ cup chopped celery
¼ cup chopped carrot
¼ cup sliced pimiento-stuffed olives
2 teaspoons capers
½ cup red wine vinegar
¼ cup water
1 tablespoon chopped fresh basil
1 tablespoon chopped fresh chives
1 tablespoon chopped fresh oregano
1 tablespoon Dijon mustard
2 cloves garlic, minced
1 teaspoon chopped fresh thyme
1 teaspoon olive oil
¼ teaspoon pepper

Cook pastas according to package directions, omitting salt and fat. Drain; rinse under cold water and drain. Place in a large bowl. Add green pepper and next 6 ingredients; toss well.

Combine vinegar and remaining ingredients in a jar; cover tightly, and shake vigorously. Pour over pasta mixture; toss well. Cover and chill thoroughly. Toss gently before serving. Yield: 8 (1-cup) servings.

PER SERVING: 141 CALORIES (10% FROM FAT)
FAT 1.6G (SATURATED FAT 0.2G)
PROTEIN 4.5G CARBOHYDRATE 26.9G
CHOLESTEROL 0MG SODIUM 227MG

BALSAMIC PASTA SALAD

¼ cup balsamic vinegar
3 tablespoons water
1½ teaspoons olive oil
¼ teaspoon salt
¼ teaspoon pepper
1 large clove garlic, minced
½ cup small broccoli flowerets
½ cup small cauliflower flowerets
½ cup julienne-cut carrot
½ cup julienne-cut sweet red pepper
4 cups cooked farfalle (bow tie pasta), cooked
   without salt or fat
2 tablespoons thinly sliced fresh basil
¼ cup grated Asiago or Parmesan cheese

Combine vinegar and next 5 ingredients in a jar; cover tightly, and shake vigorously. Set aside.

Drop broccoli, cauliflower, and carrot into a large saucepan of boiling water; cook 30 seconds. Drain. Pour cold water over broccoli mixture; drain.

Combine drained vegetables, sweet red pepper, and next 3 ingredients in a large bowl. Add vinegar mixture, and toss gently. Cover and chill. Yield: 5 (1-cup) servings.

PER SERVING: 199 CALORIES (15% FROM FAT)
FAT 3.4G (SATURATED FAT 1.1G)
PROTEIN 7.7G CARBOHYDRATE 34.3G
CHOLESTEROL 3MG SODIUM 203MG

Balsamic Pasta Salad

ORZO SALAD

1 cup orzo (rice-shaped pasta), uncooked
1 (7-ounce) jar sun-dried tomatoes in olive oil
½ cup chopped sweet red pepper
¼ cup chopped green onions
1 (4-ounce) can sliced ripe olives, drained
3 tablespoons chopped fresh parsley
¼ cup red wine vinegar
¼ teaspoon dry mustard

Cook orzo according to package directions, omitting salt and fat; drain.

Drain tomato, reserving 1 teaspoon oil. Chop 2 tablespoons tomato. Reserve remaining tomato for another use. Combine orzo, tomato, red pepper, and next 3 ingredients in a bowl; toss gently.

Combine reserved 1 teaspoon oil, vinegar, and mustard; stir well with a wire whisk. Pour over orzo mixture; toss gently. Cover and chill at least 2 hours. Yield: 8 (½-cup) servings.

PER SERVING: 116 CALORIES (12% FROM FAT)
FAT 1.5G (SATURATED FAT 0.3G)
PROTEIN 3.9G CARBOHYDRATE 22.0G
CHOLESTEROL 0MG SODIUM 154MG

FYI

Orzo is a tiny, rice-shaped pasta that can be served in place of rice as a side dish or cooked in soups and stews. Here, orzo is the main ingredient in two cold pasta salads.

ORZO-VEGETABLE SALAD IN TOMATO TULIPS

½ cup orzo (rice-shaped pasta), uncooked
½ cup frozen whole kernel corn, thawed
½ cup finely chopped carrot
½ cup finely chopped celery
½ cup diced sweet red pepper
½ cup peeled, seeded, and diced cucumber
½ cup tightly packed fresh parsley sprigs
¼ cup plain nonfat yogurt
¼ cup reduced-calorie mayonnaise
1 green onion, cut into 2-inch pieces
1 teaspoon red wine vinegar
¼ teaspoon salt
⅛ teaspoon pepper
8 medium unpeeled round red tomatoes (about 4 pounds)
Celery leaves (optional)

Cook orzo according to package directions, omitting salt and fat; drain. Combine orzo, corn, and next 4 ingredients in a large bowl; toss well.

Position knife blade in food processor bowl; add parsley and next 3 ingredients. Process 15 seconds or until smooth. Add parsley mixture, wine vinegar, salt, and pepper to orzo mixture; stir well. Cover and chill.

Core tomatoes; cut each into 4 wedges, cutting to, but not through, base of tomato. Spread wedges slightly apart, and place on 8 serving plates. Spoon orzo mixture into tomatoes. Garnish with celery leaves, if desired. Yield: 8 servings.

PER SERVING: 135 CALORIES (21% FROM FAT)
FAT 3.1G (SATURATED FAT 0.5G)
PROTEIN 4.7G CARBOHYDRATE 24.8G
CHOLESTEROL 3MG SODIUM 168MG

Orzo-Vegetable Salad in Tomato Tulips

SEASHELL SALAD

4 ounces small shell macaroni, uncooked
⅓ cup plain low-fat yogurt
2 teaspoons lemon juice
2 teaspoons olive oil
½ teaspoon dried whole dillweed
¼ teaspoon salt
⅛ teaspoon garlic powder
⅛ teaspoon white pepper
1 cup frozen English peas, thawed and drained
½ cup thinly sliced cauliflower flowerets
¼ cup finely chopped celery
¼ cup shredded carrot
8 lettuce leaves

Cook macaroni according to package directions, omitting salt and fat. Drain; rinse with cold water, and drain again. Cover and chill.

Combine yogurt and next 6 ingredients, stirring with a wire whisk. Cover and chill. Combine peas, cauliflower, celery, and carrot; toss gently. Add macaroni and yogurt mixture; toss gently. Cover and chill. Serve on lettuce-lined salad plates. Yield: 8 servings.

PER SERVING: 91 CALORIES (16% FROM FAT)
FAT 1.6G (SATURATED FAT 0.3G)
PROTEIN 3.7G CARBOHYDRATE 15.1G
CHOLESTEROL 1MG SODIUM 105MG

MACARONI SALAD

⅓ cup peeled, diced cucumber
2 tablespoons white vinegar
4 cups cooked elbow macaroni (cooked without salt or fat)
½ cup chopped green pepper
⅓ cup thinly sliced celery
¼ cup sliced green onions
1 (2-ounce) jar diced pimiento, drained
½ cup plain low-fat yogurt
¼ cup reduced-calorie mayonnaise
¾ teaspoon dry mustard
½ teaspoon salt
½ teaspoon dried whole dillweed
⅛ teaspoon pepper

Combine cucumber and vinegar in a medium bowl; let stand 30 minutes. Add macaroni and next 4 ingredients; toss well. Combine yogurt and next 5 ingredients; stir well. Add to macaroni mixture; toss gently to coat. Cover and chill. Yield: 12 (½-cup) servings.

PER SERVING: 89 CALORIES (19% FROM FAT)
FAT 1.9G (SATURATED FAT 0.3G)
PROTEIN 3.0G CARBOHYDRATE 15.1G
CHOLESTEROL 2MG SODIUM 147MG

CHILLED BROCCOLI-PASTA SALAD

Thinly sliced red cabbage adds a unique texture and color to this pasta salad.

3 cups fresh broccoli flowerets
3 cups cooked rotini (corkscrew pasta), cooked without salt or fat
1 cup thinly sliced red cabbage
1 clove garlic
2 teaspoons sugar
¼ teaspoon pepper
3 tablespoons white wine vinegar
3 tablespoons commercial mango chutney
1 tablespoon Dijon mustard
2 tablespoons vegetable oil

Drop broccoli into a large saucepan of boiling water; return to a boil. Cook 1 minute; drain. Pour cold water over broccoli; drain. Combine broccoli, pasta, and cabbage in a large bowl; set aside.

Place garlic in container of an electric blender; cover and process until minced. Add sugar and next 4 ingredients; cover and process until smooth. With blender running, add oil through opening in lid; process until blended. Pour over pasta mixture; toss gently. Cover and chill 30 minutes. Yield: 5 (1-cup) servings.

PER SERVING: 217 CALORIES (27% FROM FAT)
FAT 6.4G (SATURATED FAT 1.1G)
PROTEIN 5.8G CARBOHYDRATE 34.8G
CHOLESTEROL 0MG SODIUM 127MG

COLORFUL VEGETABLE SALAD

¼ cup sliced carrots
1½ cups fresh broccoli flowerets
1 (14-ounce) can artichoke hearts, drained and quartered
3 cups cooked fusilli (corkscrew pasta), cooked without salt or fat
Parmesan-Garlic Dressing
1¼ cups cherry tomato halves
8 lettuce leaves

Place carrot in a vegetable steamer over boiling water. Cover and steam 3 minutes. Add broccoli; cover and steam an additional 5 minutes or until crisp-tender. Combine carrot mixture, artichoke hearts, pasta, and Parmesan-Garlic Dressing in a large bowl; toss gently to coat. Chill at least 1 hour.

To serve, add cherry tomatoes; toss gently. Serve on lettuce-lined plates. Yield: 8 (1-cup) servings.

PARMESAN-GARLIC DRESSING
½ cup plain low-fat yogurt
¼ cup red wine vinegar
2 tablespoons grated Parmesan cheese
2 tablespoons reduced-calorie mayonnaise
¼ teaspoon garlic powder
¼ teaspoon pepper
⅛ teaspoon salt

Combine all ingredients in container of an electric blender; cover and process at low speed until smooth. Yield: 1 cup.

PER SERVING: 143 CALORIES (20% FROM FAT)
FAT 3.1G (SATURATED FAT 0.8G)
PROTEIN 6.4G CARBOHYDRATE 25.3G
CHOLESTEROL 3MG SODIUM 152MG

VEGETABLE SALAD WITH PASTA WHEELS

2 cups cooked wagon wheel pasta (cooked without salt or fat)
1 cup drained canned pinto beans
1 (8-ounce) package frozen Sugar Snap peas, thawed and diagonally sliced in half
2 tablespoons sliced green onions
⅓ cup plain nonfat yogurt
3 tablespoons reduced-calorie mayonnaise
½ teaspoon dried whole tarragon
¼ teaspoon salt
¼ teaspoon cracked pepper
5 large red leaf lettuce leaves
5 plum tomatoes, each cut into 6 wedges
20 diagonally-cut slices peeled, seedless cucumber

Combine first 4 ingredients in a large bowl; set aside. Combine yogurt and next 4 ingredients in a bowl, stirring with a wire whisk until blended. Pour over pasta mixture; toss gently.

Spoon onto individual lettuce-lined salad plates; arrange tomato and cucumber on top of salads. Yield: 5 (1-cup) servings.

PER SERVING: 188 CALORIES (17% FROM FAT)
FAT 3.5G (SATURATED FAT 0.2G)
PROTEIN 8.0G CARBOHYDRATE 31.4G
CHOLESTEROL 3MG SODIUM 280MG

FYI

Store dried herbs away from heat, light, and air, and they will retain their flavors for 6 to 12 months. For longer storage, you can store dried herbs in the freezer.

Caesar Salad with Tortellini

CAESAR SALAD WITH TORTELLINI

3 tablespoons fresh lemon juice
2 tablespoons water
1 tablespoon olive oil
1 teaspoon anchovy paste
⅛ teaspoon freshly ground pepper
1 clove garlic, crushed
9 ounces fresh cheese tortellini, uncooked
1½ cups (2-inch pieces) fresh asparagus
   (about 1 pound)
12 cups loosely packed torn romaine lettuce
¼ cup freshly grated Parmesan cheese

Combine first 6 ingredients in a bowl; stir well with a wire whisk. Set aside.

Cook tortellini in boiling water 7 minutes or until tender, omitting salt and fat. Drain well, and set aside.

Arrange asparagus in a vegetable steamer over boiling water. Cover and steam 2 minutes or until crisp-tender. Combine asparagus and tortellini in a bowl; add 2 tablespoons lemon juice mixture, tossing gently to coat.

Place lettuce in a large bowl; drizzle remaining lemon juice mixture over lettuce, and toss well. Add tortellini mixture, tossing gently. Spoon salad onto individual serving plates; sprinkle with cheese. Yield: 6 servings.

PER SERVING: 223 CALORIES (33% FROM FAT)
FAT 8.1G (SATURATED FAT 2.9G)
PROTEIN 12.7G   CARBOHYDRATE 24.9G
CHOLESTEROL 26MG   SODIUM 430MG

PASTA AND VEGETABLE SALAD

2½ cups cooked fresh spinach tortellini with
    cheese (cooked without salt or fat)
1 cup sliced zucchini
1 cup sweet red pepper strips
1 cup sweet yellow pepper strips
½ cup thinly sliced purple onion
3 tablespoons white wine vinegar
2 tablespoons water
1 tablespoon olive oil
2 teaspoons Dijon mustard
⅛ teaspoon pepper
Dash of crushed red pepper
1 clove garlic, minced

    Combine tortellini and next 4 ingredients in a
bowl, and toss well.
    Combine vinegar and next 6 ingredients in a jar.
Cover tightly, and shake vigorously. Drizzle over
tortellini mixture, tossing gently to coat. Yield: 8
(1-cup) servings.

PER SERVING: 102 CALORIES (27% FROM FAT)
FAT 3.1G (SATURATED FAT 0.8G)
PROTEIN 4.6G   CARBOHYDRATE 14.3G
CHOLESTEROL 11MG   SODIUM 131MG

TORTELLINI SALAD

1½ cups fresh broccoli flowerets
½ cup thinly sliced carrot
3 cups cooked fresh cheese tortellini (cooked
    without salt or fat)
½ cup diced sweet red pepper
½ cup diced sweet yellow pepper
1 tablespoon minced purple onion
¼ cup red wine vinegar
1 tablespoon olive oil
1 teaspoon Dijon mustard
¾ teaspoon dried whole basil
¼ teaspoon pepper
⅛ teaspoon salt
1 clove garlic, minced

    Arrange broccoli flowerets and carrot in a veg-
etable steamer over boiling water. Cover and steam
3 minutes or until vegetables are crisp-tender.
Plunge into cold water and drain.
    Combine broccoli mixture, tortellini, red and yellow
peppers, and purple onion in a large bowl, and toss well.
    Combine vinegar and next 6 ingredients in a bowl,
and stir well. Pour over tortellini mixture, and toss gently to coat. Cover and chill. Yield: 5 (1-cup) servings.

PER SERVING: 258 CALORIES (22% FROM FAT)
FAT 6.2G (SATURATED FAT 2.0G)
PROTEIN 13.3G   CARBOHYDRATE 50.9G
CHOLESTEROL 31MG   SODIUM 410MG

EGG-ORZO SALAD

1 cup orzo (rice-shaped pasta), uncooked
1 cup chopped green pepper
½ cup diced purple onion
½ cup frozen English peas, thawed
¼ cup chopped fresh parsley
1 tablespoon dried dillweed
¼ cup plus 2 tablespoons plain low-fat yogurt
2 tablespoons reduced-calorie salad dressing or
    mayonnaise
2 tablespoons Dijon mustard
¼ teaspoon salt
¼ teaspoon pepper
3 drops hot sauce
12 leaf lettuce leaves
4 hard-cooked eggs, each sliced into 6 wedges
Radish fans (optional)
Cucumber slices (optional)

    Cook orzo according to package directions, omit-
ting salt and fat. Combine orzo and next 5 ingredients in a large bowl; toss gently. Combine yogurt
and next 5 ingredients; stir well. Add to orzo mixture, stirring gently. Cover and chill.
    To serve, spoon onto 6 lettuce-lined plates.
Arrange eggs on side of each salad. Garnish with
radishes and cucumber, if desired. Yield: 6 servings.

PER SERVING: 241 CALORIES (23% FROM FAT)
FAT 6.2G (SATURATED FAT 1.3G)
PROTEIN 11.3G   CARBOHYDRATE 34.2G
CHOLESTEROL 150MG   SODIUM 348MG

TROPICAL FRUIT AND PASTA SALAD

3 cups cooked fusilli (corkscrew pasta),
   cooked without salt or fat
Yogurt-Poppyseed Dressing
1 cup fresh pineapple tidbits
1 cup sliced fresh strawberries
¾ cup peeled, cubed mango
⅓ cup peeled, cubed kiwifruit (about 1 medium)
Red leaf lettuce leaves (optional)

Combine pasta and ¼ cup Yogurt-Poppyseed Dressing in a large bowl, tossing gently to coat. Cover and chill 1 hour.

To serve, add remaining dressing and next 4 ingredients to pasta mixture; toss gently. Serve on lettuce, if desired. Yield: 8 (¾-cup) servings.

YOGURT-POPPYSEED DRESSING
¾ cup plain low-fat yogurt
1 tablespoon unsweetened pineapple juice
1 tablespoon honey
½ teaspoon poppy seeds
⅛ teaspoon ground nutmeg

Combine all ingredients in a small bowl; stir well. Cover and chill 2 hours. Yield: ¾ cup.

PER SERVING: 129 CALORIES (12% FROM FAT)
FAT 1.7G (SATURATED FAT 0.4G)
PROTEIN 4.3G   CARBOHYDRATE 26.3G
CHOLESTEROL 1MG   SODIUM 16MG

FUSILLI FRUIT SALAD

Feel free to use a different yogurt such as pineapple or apricot.

3 ounces fusilli (corkscrew pasta), uncooked
1 (8-ounce) can unsweetened pineapple
   chunks, undrained
1 cup cantaloupe chunks
1 cup seedless green grapes, halved
1 (8-ounce) carton peach low-fat yogurt
1 cup strawberry halves
Lettuce leaves (optional)

Cook pasta according to package directions, omitting salt and fat. Drain; rinse with cold water, and drain again.

Drain pineapple, reserving 2 tablespoons juice. Combine pasta, pineapple chunks, cantaloupe, and grapes in a medium bowl. Cover and chill.

Combine yogurt and reserved 2 tablespoons pineapple juice in a small bowl, stirring well. Cover yogurt mixture and chill.

Add strawberry halves to pasta mixture just before serving; toss gently. Transfer mixture to a lettuce-lined serving bowl, if desired. Drizzle yogurt mixture over pasta salad, and serve immediately. Yield: 8 servings.

PER SERVING: 112 CALORIES (6% FROM FAT)
FAT 0.7G (SATURATED FAT 0.3G)
PROTEIN 2.9G   CARBOHYDRATE 24.1G
CHOLESTEROL 1MG   SODIUM 18MG

FYI

If you don't have enough of any particular pasta shape for your recipe, just mix what you have. Combine similar sizes so that each of the types will be done at the same time. (See page 7 for interchangeable pasta shapes.)

Fusilli Fruit Salad

CHINESE CHICKEN PASTA SALAD

2 cups shredded cooked chicken breast (about
   1 pound skinned, boned chicken breast)
2 cups cooked radiatore (short, fat rippled
   pasta), cooked without salt or fat
1½ cups diagonally sliced (½-inch) fresh snow
   pea pods
½ cup diced sweet red pepper
¼ cup sliced green onions
1 (8-ounce) can sliced water chestnuts,
   drained
⅓ cup plain low-fat yogurt
2½ tablespoons low-sodium soy sauce
2 tablespoons reduced-calorie mayonnaise
¼ teaspoon pepper
⅛ teaspoon ground ginger
1 tablespoon plus 2 teaspoons slivered
   almonds, toasted

Combine first 6 ingredients in a large bowl; toss
gently, and set aside.

Combine yogurt and next 4 ingredients in a bowl;
stir well. Add to chicken mixture; toss gently to coat.
Sprinkle with almonds. Yield: 4 (1½-cup) servings.

PER SERVING: 375 CALORIES (18% FROM FAT)
FAT 7.3G (SATURATED FAT 1.8G)
PROTEIN 33.6G CARBOHYDRATE 40.6G
CHOLESTEROL 76MG SODIUM 388MG

Menu Helper

Try jazzing up your carry-along lunches with
a special salad. Designed to supercharge the
body and mind, these are full of flavor but low
in fat. Just add crackers and fruit to either of
these chicken salads for a complete meal.
Remember to keep the salad cool by storing it
in the refrigerator or in an insulated lunchbox.

CHICKEN-PASTA SALAD DELUXE

8 ounces small farfalle (bow tie pasta),
   uncooked
1 pound skinned, boned chicken breast halves
Vegetable cooking spray
1 teaspoon vegetable oil
¼ teaspoon paprika
1 cup water
¾ pound fresh broccoli, cut into 1-inch pieces
1 cup unsweetened orange juice
¼ cup plus 2 tablespoons cider vinegar
1 teaspoon ground ginger
½ teaspoon paprika
¼ teaspoon pepper
4 medium oranges, peeled, sectioned, and seeded
¼ cup sliced almonds, toasted

Cook pasta according to package directions, omitting salt and fat. Drain and set aside in a large bowl.

Cut chicken into 3- x ½-inch strips. Coat a large
skillet with cooking spray; add oil. Place over medium heat until hot. Add chicken, and sauté 5 minutes or until chicken is tender. Stir in ¼ teaspoon
paprika during last minute of cooking time. Add
chicken to pasta. Cover and chill. Wipe drippings
from skillet with a paper towel.

Add water to skillet; bring to a boil. Add broccoli.
Cover; reduce heat, and simmer 3 minutes or until
broccoli is crisp-tender. Drain well, and set aside to
cool; chill.

Combine orange juice and next 4 ingredients in a
small bowl; stir until well blended. Pour over pasta
mixture; add orange sections, and toss gently.
Cover and chill thoroughly.

Add broccoli and almonds just before serving,
tossing gently. Serve chilled. Yield: 8 servings.

PER SERVING: 257 CALORIES (15% FROM FAT)
FAT 4.4G (SATURATED FAT 0.8G)
PROTEIN 19.2G CARBOHYDRATE 36.0G
CHOLESTEROL 35MG SODIUM 45MG

DILLED TURKEY SALAD

Elbow macaroni and wagon wheel pasta are good substitutes for the shells in this salad.

6 ounces shell macaroni, uncooked
¾ pound cooked turkey breast, cut into strips
2 cups chopped tomato
½ cup diced celery
¼ cup minced red onion
¼ cup chopped fresh parsley
1 tablespoon plus 2 teaspoons red wine vinegar
1 tablespoon vegetable oil
2 teaspoons grated Parmesan cheese
1½ teaspoons dried whole dillweed
2 cloves garlic, minced
½ teaspoon pepper
¼ teaspoon salt

Cook macaroni according to package directions, omitting salt and fat. Drain well. Rinse pasta under cold water; drain.

Combine cooked pasta, turkey, tomato, celery, onion, and parsley in a large bowl; toss well. Combine vinegar and remaining ingredients in a small bowl, stirring well. Pour vinegar mixture over pasta mixture; toss gently to combine. Cover and chill at least 2 hours. Yield: 8 (1-cup) servings.

PER SERVING: 285 CALORIES (12% FROM FAT)
FAT 3.9G (SATURATED FAT 1.0G)
PROTEIN 15.8G   CARBOHYDRATE 43.3G
CHOLESTEROL 7MG   SODIUM 443MG

SCALLOP AND PASTA SALAD

1½ pounds fresh bay scallops, halved
½ cup lemon juice
½ cup lime juice
12 ounces small shell macaroni, uncooked
1 teaspoon vegetable oil
1 cup diced sweet red pepper
1 cup diced green pepper
¼ cup chopped fresh cilantro
2 tablespoons diced purple onion
1 jalapeño pepper, seeded and minced
¼ cup water
2 tablespoons rice vinegar
1 teaspoon olive oil
1 teaspoon Dijon mustard
¼ teaspoon salt
⅛ teaspoon pepper
Fresh cilantro sprigs (optional)

Place scallops in boiling water to cover; reduce heat, and simmer 4 minutes. Drain. Transfer scallops to a glass bowl. Pour lemon juice and lime juice over scallops. Cover and marinate in refrigerator 4 to 6 hours.

Cook macaroni according to package directions, omitting salt and fat; drain. Rinse with cold water, and drain again. Place macaroni in a large bowl. Add vegetable oil; toss gently.

Drain scallops; add scallops, sweet red pepper, and next 4 ingredients to macaroni. Combine water, vinegar, olive oil, mustard, salt, and pepper; stir with a wire whisk until blended. Pour over macaroni mixture, and toss gently. Garnish with fresh cilantro sprigs, if desired. Serve immediately. Yield: 12 (1-cup) servings.

PER SERVING: 175 CALORIES (9% FROM FAT)
FAT 1.8G (SATURATED FAT 0.2G)
PROTEIN 13.4G   CARBOHYDRATE 25.4G
CHOLESTEROL 19MG   SODIUM 155MG

Mexican Shrimp and Pasta Salad

Mexican Shrimp and Pasta Salad

¾ pound unpeeled medium-size fresh shrimp
1 teaspoon ground cumin
¼ teaspoon chili powder
Vegetable cooking spray
1 teaspoon olive oil
½ cup canned no-salt-added chicken broth, undiluted
1 small avocado, peeled and coarsely chopped
1 cup chopped fresh cilantro
¼ cup chopped green onions
3 tablespoons lime juice
1 large jalapeño pepper, seeded and chopped
1 clove garlic
6 ounces fettuccine, uncooked
¼ cup sliced ripe olives
¼ cup shredded zucchini
2 tablespoons chopped tomato
Avocado slices (optional)
Fresh cilantro sprigs (optional)

Peel and devein shrimp. Sprinkle shrimp evenly with cumin and chili powder. Coat a large nonstick skillet with cooking spray; add oil. Place over medium heat until hot. Add shrimp; sauté 3 to 5 minutes or until done. Drain shrimp, and pat dry with paper towels; cover and chill. Wipe skillet dry with a paper towel.

Add broth to skillet; bring to a boil, and cook until reduced to ¼ cup. Remove from heat; let cool. Pour broth into container of an electric blender. Add avocado and next 5 ingredients; cover and process until smooth.

Cook fettuccine according to package directions, omitting salt and fat; drain. Rinse under cold water; drain well. Combine fettuccine and one-third of avocado mixture; toss well. Place fettuccine in center of a serving platter. Top with shrimp, olives, zucchini, tomato, and remaining avocado mixture. Garnish with avocado slices and fresh cilantro sprigs, if desired. Yield: 4 servings.

Per Serving: 322 Calories (28% from fat)
Fat 10.0g (Saturated Fat 1.6g)
Protein 21.7g Carbohydrate 36.9g
Cholesterol 112mg Sodium 199mg

Shrimp-Pasta Salad

4 cups cooked small shell macaroni (cooked without salt or fat)
1½ cups chopped cooked fresh shrimp (about 1 pound)
½ cup frozen English peas, thawed
½ cup sliced green onions
¼ cup chopped fresh parsley
½ cup plain low-fat yogurt
½ cup reduced-calorie mayonnaise
2 tablespoons chopped fresh dillweed
2 teaspoons grated lemon rind
2 tablespoons fresh lemon juice
¼ teaspoon salt
⅛ teaspoon pepper

Combine first 5 ingredients in a large bowl; toss well. Combine yogurt and next 6 ingredients in a bowl; stir well. Add to pasta mixture, tossing to coat. Cover and chill. Yield: 6 (1-cup) servings.

Per Serving: 249 Calories (24% from fat)
Fat 6.7g (Saturated Fat 0.7g)
Protein 15.3g Carbohydrate 31.1g
Cholesterol 91mg Sodium 373mg

Tuna Salad Primavera

3 cups cooked medium shell macaroni (cooked without salt or fat)
1 cup julienne-cut sweet red pepper
½ cup sliced carrot
½ cup frozen English peas, thawed
¼ cup thinly sliced green onions
1 (9¼-ounce) can chunk light tuna in water, drained
½ cup commercial oil-free Italian dressing

Combine pasta and next 5 ingredients in a bowl; toss gently. Add dressing; toss well. Cover and chill. Yield: 4 servings.

Per Serving: 247 Calories (7% from fat)
Fat 2.0 g (Saturated Fat 0.4g)
Protein 18.3g Carbohydrate 37.7g
Cholesterol 19mg Sodium 527mg

PASTA NIÇOISE

8 ounces rotini (corkscrew pasta), uncooked
2 teaspoons olive oil
¼ teaspoon dried red pepper flakes
¼ pound fresh green beans
¾ cup chopped fresh parsley
½ cup chopped purple onion
½ cup sliced ripe olives
16 cherry tomatoes, quartered
1 medium-size green pepper, seeded and
    chopped
1 clove garlic, minced
2 tablespoons red wine vinegar
2 teaspoons olive oil
1 tablespoon grated Parmesan cheese
1 teaspoon dried whole oregano
⅛ teaspoon pepper
1 (6½-ounce) can water-packed tuna

Cook pasta according to package directions, omitting salt and fat; drain. Rinse with cold water, and drain again. Combine pasta, 2 teaspoons olive oil, and red pepper flakes in a large bowl; toss well, and set aside.

Wash green beans; trim ends, and remove strings. Cut beans diagonally into 1-inch pieces. Place beans in a vegetable steamer over boiling water. Cover and steam 2 minutes or until crisp-tender. Let beans cool completely.

Combine beans, parsley, and next 10 ingredients in a large bowl; toss well.

Place tuna in a colander, and rinse under cold running water 1 minute; set aside to drain 1 minute. Add tuna to bean mixture, tossing gently.

Transfer pasta mixture to a serving platter; spoon tuna mixture over pasta. Yield: 4 servings.

PER SERVING: 377 CALORIES (21% FROM FAT)
FAT 8.6G (SATURATED FAT 1.6G)
PROTEIN 22.9G   CARBOHYDRATE 52.5G
CHOLESTEROL 31MG   SODIUM 602MG

TUNA AND PASTA SALAD

(pictured on page 122)

8 ounces penne (tubular pasta), uncooked
¾ cup water
3 tablespoons olive oil
2 tablespoons balsamic vinegar
1 teaspoon dried whole oregano
¼ teaspoon ground white pepper
⅛ teaspoon salt
1 (14-ounce) can artichoke hearts, drained and
    quartered
1 (9¼-ounce) can water-packed tuna, drained
2 cups shredded romaine lettuce
12 cherry tomatoes, halved
Red leaf lettuce (optional)

Cook pasta according to package directions, omitting salt and fat; drain. Place pasta in a large bowl, and set aside.

Combine water and next 5 ingredients in a small bowl; stir with a wire whisk. Pour ½ cup vinegar mixture over pasta; toss. Add remaining vinegar mixture, artichoke hearts, tuna, lettuce, and tomatoes; toss. Cover and chill. Serve on lettuce-lined salad plates, if desired. Yield: 10 (1-cup) servings.

PER SERVING: 160 CALORIES (26% FROM FAT)
FAT 4.7G (SATURATED FAT 0.6G)
PROTEIN 8.9G   CARBOHYDRATE 20.0G
CHOLESTEROL 6MG   SODIUM 117MG

Lighten Up

Canned tuna comes in several varieties—tuna packed in water or oil, chunk or solid pack, light tuna or white albacore tuna. Tuna packed in water rather than oil nets a 60 percent savings in calories; that is, 60 calories versus 150 calories per 2-ounce serving (about ¼ cup). White albacore tuna has a milder taste and lighter color than light tuna, making it the preferred choice for delicately flavored dishes.

INDEX

METRIC EQUIVALENTS

Metric Equivalents for Different Types of Ingredients

A standard cup measure of a dry or solid ingredient will vary in weight depending on the type of ingredient. A standard cup of liquid is the same volume for any type of liquid. Use the following chart when converting standard cup measures to grams (weight) or milliliters (volume).

Standard Cup	Fine Powder (ex. flour)	Grain (ex. rice)	Granular (ex. sugar)	Liquid Solids (ex. butter)	Liquid (ex. milk)
1	140 g	150 g	190 g	200 g	240 ml
¾	105 g	113 g	143 g	150 g	180 ml
⅔	93 g	100 g	125 g	133 g	160 ml
½	70 g	75 g	95 g	100 g	120 ml
⅓	47 g	50 g	63 g	67 g	80 ml
¼	35 g	38 g	48 g	50 g	60 ml
⅛	18 g	19 g	24 g	25 g	30 ml

Useful Equivalents for Liquid Ingredients by Volume

¼ tsp					=	1 ml
½ tsp					=	2 ml
1 tsp					=	5 ml
3 tsp	=	1 tbls		=	½ fl oz	=	15 ml
		2 tbls	=	⅛ cup	=	1 fl oz	=	30 ml
		4 tbls	=	¼ cup	=	2 fl oz	=	60 ml
		5⅓ tbls	=	⅓ cup	=	3 fl oz	=	80 ml
		8 tbls	=	½ cup	=	4 fl oz	=	120 ml
		10⅔ tbls	=	⅔ cup	=	5 fl oz	=	160 ml
		12 tbls	=	¾ cup	=	6 fl oz	=	180 ml
		16 tbls	=	1 cup	=	8 fl oz	=	240 ml
		1 pt	=	2 cups	=	16 fl oz	=	480 ml
		1 qt	=	4 cups	=	32 fl oz	=	960 ml
						33 fl oz	=	1000 ml = 1 l

Useful Equivalents for Dry Ingredients by Weight

(To convert ounces to grams, multiply the number of ounces by 30.)

1 oz	=	¹⁄₁₆ lb	=	30 g
4 oz	=	¼ lb	=	120 g
8 oz	=	½ lb	=	240 g
12 oz	=	¾ lb	=	360 g
16 oz	=	1 lb	=	480 g

Useful Equivalents for Cooking/Oven Temperatures

	Fahrenheit	Celcius	Gas Mark
Freeze Water	32° F	0° C	
Room Temperature	68° F	20° C	
Boil Water	212° F	100° C	
Bake	325° F	160° C	3
	350° F	180° C	4
	375° F	190° C	5
	400° F	200° C	6
	425° F	220° C	7
	450° F	230° C	8
Broil			Grill

Useful Equivalents for Length

(To convert inches to centimeters, multiply the number of inches by 2.5.)

1 in					=	2.5 cm
6 in	=	½ ft			=	15 cm
12 in	=	1 ft			=	30 cm
36 in	=	3 ft	=	1 yd	=	90 cm
40 in					=	100 cm = 1 m